Disrupting Investigative Journalism

This book makes the case for the enormous potential embodied in investigative journalism if reporters collaborate in the digital sphere and engage with emerging techniques and technologies.

Bringing together personal narratives from investigative journalists who have successfully found, verified and published stories using social media platforms and Web based communications, *Disrupting Investigative Journalism* explores the risks and benefits that come from this kind of digital collaboration. Citing how digital connection has enabled reporters around the world to form the International Consortium of Investigative Journalists, which in turn led to such global news sensations as the Panama Papers and the Paradise Papers, this book makes a practical argument for how the daily work of investigative journalism can change to capture enormous latent potential.

This is a valuable text for students and scholars in the fields of investigative journalism, media and digital communication.

Amanda Gearing is an award-winning investigative journalist, author and broadcaster. She holds a PhD in Investigative Journalism from Queensland University of Technology, Australia.

T0347545

Disruptions: Studies in Digital Journalism
Series editor: Bob Franklin

Disruptions refers to the radical changes provoked by the affordances of digital technologies that occur at a pace and on a scale that disrupts settled understandings and traditional ways of creating value, interacting and communicating both socially and professionally. The consequences for digital journalism involve far reaching changes to business models, professional practices, roles, ethics, products and even challenges to the accepted definitions and understandings of journalism. For Digital Journalism Studies, the field of academic inquiry which explores and examines digital journalism, disruption results in paradigmatic and tectonic shifts in scholarly concerns. It prompts reconsideration of research methods, theoretical analyses and responses (oppositional and consensual) to such changes, which have been described as being akin to 'a moment of mind-blowing uncertainty.'

Routledge's new book series, *Disruptions: Studies in Digital Journalism*, seeks to capture, examine and analyse these moments of exciting and explosive professional and scholarly innovation which characterize developments in the day-to-day practice of journalism in an age of digital media, and which are articulated in the newly emerging academic discipline of Digital Journalism Studies.

Disrupting Investigative Journalism
Moment of Death or Dramatic Rebirth?
Amanda Gearing

Journalism Education for the Digital Age
Promises, Perils, and Possibilities
Brian Creech

Transparency and Journalism
A Critical Appraisal of a Disruptive Norm
Michael Karlsson

For more information, please visit:
www.routledge.com/Disruptions/book-series/DISRUPTDIGJOUR

Disrupting Investigative Journalism

Moment of Death or Dramatic Rebirth?

Amanda Gearing

Routledge
Taylor & Francis Group

LONDON AND NEW YORK

First published 2021
by Routledge
2 Park Square, Milton Park, Abingdon, Oxon OX14 4RN

and by Routledge
605 Third Avenue, New York, NY 10158

Routledge is an imprint of the Taylor & Francis Group, an informa business

British Library Cataloguing-in-Publication Data
A catalogue record for this book is available from the British Library

Library of Congress Cataloging-in-Publication Data
Names: Gearing, Amanda, author.
Title: Disrupting investigative journalism : moment of death or dramatic rebirth? / Amanda Gearing.
Description: Abingdon, Oxon ; New York : Routledge, 2021. | Series: Disruptions | Includes bibliographical references and index.
Identifiers: LCCN 2021003595 (print) |
LCCN 2021003596 (ebook) | ISBN 9780367690014 (hardback) | ISBN 9780367690038 (paperback) | ISBN 9781003139980 (ebook)
Subjects: LCSH: Investigative reporting. |
Journalism--Technological innovations. | Online journalism.
Classification: LCC PN4781 .G43 2021 (print) | LCC PN4781 (ebook) | DDC 070.4/3–dc23
LC record available at https://lccn.loc.gov/2021003595
LC ebook record available at https://lccn.loc.gov/2021003596

ISBN: 9780367690014 (hbk)
ISBN: 9780367690038 (pbk)
ISBN: 9781003139980 (ebk)

DOI: 10.4324/9781003139980

Typeset in Times New Roman
by Taylor & Francis Books

To Denis Butler, whose investigation and feature writing inspired me to become a journalist.

Contents

Figures

Preface

Investigative journalism stands at a pivotal moment when the profession risks turning aside from its mandate to constitute a fourth estate because of digital disruption, lack of funds, legal constraints and other challenges. The proud and important history of investigative journalism as a watchdog for democracy, a voice for the voiceless and the driving force behind reforming legislation is at risk of losing its potency.

My aim in this book is to take readers behind the headlines and into the daily life of leading investigative journalists, who are working successfully in the disrupted media landscape using new techniques and technologies as well as traditional skills to continue their important role. This book draws substantially on the primary research findings of my PhD 'Global investigative journalism in the Digital Age' completed at the Queensland University of Technology in Brisbane in 2016. The journalists who contributed to the study have learned how to save time, money and travel by developing novel ways to find, verify and publish important and revelatory news coverage. They have generously shared their skills and experience with me. It is my privilege to present and appraise their work – along with some of my own – in the hope of inspiring new generations of investigative reporters in their careers. Digital disruption undoubtedly poses significant challenges but also presents enormous opportunities. The power of hyper-connectivity via internet-enabled communications is limited only by the limits of our imagination.

At a time of global challenges including the COVID pandemic and climate change, collaboration between reporters around the world can provide a beacon of hope that humanity will be able to examine and address its collective problems. Investigative journalism is not an easy career but it can be extraordinarily satisfying to be an instrument of change for the betterment of humankind.

Acknowledgements

I am grateful to the many investigative journalists who shared their insights, joys and challenges as digitisation disrupted the analogue methods used in our work over decades. Their contributions provide a foundation for understanding what is happening at the coalface of investigative journalism at a time of revolutionary change in the industry. The reporters, cameramen, technical staff and news sources who contributed to this research are: Vivien Altman, Bim Atkinson, Michael Bachelard, Richard Baker, James Campbell, Matt Carr, Ben Doherty, Caro Meldrum-Hanna, Joanne McCarthy, Michael McKenna, Donna Page, Madhvi Pankhania, Darren Pateman, Nicky Phillips, Mandy Squires, Gerard Ryle, Eli Ward and Sarah Whyte.

I am particularly grateful to whistleblowers Eli Ward and to Bim Atkinson for their courage in being willing to step into the international media spotlight at a time of personal vulnerability and challenge. In addition to the media coverage, both men were also willing to describe their experience of being the subject of media coverage that was simultaneously confronting and liberating for them.

A project such as this does not happen without inspiration, guidance and encouragement. Thanks are owed to my academic mentors at the Queensland University of Technology, Professor Brian McNair, Associate Professor Leo Bowman and Professor Folker Hanusch who oversaw my research. Thanks also to Dr Peter Berglez for research collaboration on other projects. Finally, and most profoundly, to my husband Phillip for practical help and support, please accept my heartfelt thanks.

Thank you to Bob Franklin for inviting my participation in the Disruptions Series. It has been a joy to work with you. I am honoured to contribute to this important corpus of work.

1 Analogue to digital

Ophthalmologist Dr Li Wenliang wrote a social media post in a doctor's chat group at Wuhan Central Hospital at the end of December 2019. He alerted his colleagues to seven cases of a viral infection similar to severe acute respiratory syndrome (SARS) and warned them to wear protective clothing.[1] On 4 January, the doctor was summoned to the Public Security Bureau where he was told to sign a letter. In the letter he was accused of "making false comments" that had "severely disturbed the social order":

> We solemnly warn you: If you keep being stubborn, with such impertinence, and continue this illegal activity, you will be brought to justice – is that understood?

Underneath in Dr Li's handwriting is written: "Yes, I do."[2]

Dr Li had unwittingly identified a novel coronavirus that was poised to spread around the globe, infecting tens of millions of people and potentially killing millions of people.[3] Dr Li's warning of the onset of what became COVID-19 came three weeks before China ordered the city of Wuhan to be locked down on 23 January 2020. Dr Li was a brave whistleblower who possessed information that he knew was important to his society and to humanity. His national government did not fully understand what was happening but tried to silence his voice. History now records the importance of this medically trained whistleblower saying what he said at the time he alerted his colleagues. Had this scenario played out a few years earlier in the analogue age, it is unlikely Dr Li's chat with colleagues would have become world news. Digitisation and social media enabled his discovery to be shared, despite the risks. His brave action illustrates why it matters so much that investigative journalism is currently facing a death threat and why it needs a dramatic rebirth.

Dr Li's private comment documented the beginning of what quickly became a global pandemic. Even when the Chinese authorities tried to

DOI: 10.4324/9781003139980-1

silence him, Dr Li released documentary evidence of those attempts. Despite the risk of official sanctions, he posted a letter to a social media chat group and documented his last illness from 10 January when he started coughing; next day, when he had a fever; and two days later when he was admitted to hospital. The outbreak of a novel coronavirus was officially declared on 20 January. Dr Li was diagnosed on 30 January. The Public Security Bureau sent him a written apology, which Dr Li also shared with his colleagues. Dr Li had only one week to live but he lived to see the disease he discovered recognised by global health authorities. The following day, 31 January 2020, the World Health Organisation declared a global health emergency as the outbreak spread beyond China and raised fears for populations in other countries, especially countries with poor health systems.[4] In China, at least 213 people had already died of the illness and around 10,000 new cases were being reported each day.[5] The Chinese authorities ordered people to stay inside.[6] *BBC News* published details of the doctor's medical discovery on 6 February 2020. Dr Li died the following day, 7 February 2020, aged 33 (Green 2020). China closed air, train and road transport in and out of Wuhan and nearby cities, isolating an estimated 760 million people in their homes (Cyranoski 2020).

Investigative journalism is the means by which the voices of whistle-blowers such as Dr Li are heard, verified and then amplified via media outlets. Publication and broadcast of the information enables everyone who needs to know the information to hear and to respond. It allows members of the public to take action for themselves and their families. It alerts local, state and national governments to respond to protect their citizens from external or internal threats or opportunities. It allows the global community to respond to assist groups of people or nations that need financial or logistical assistance to be able to protect their people.

The necessity of investigative journalism is further underlined by the consequences of the three-week delay in officially declaring the emergence of a deadly and highly infectious novel virus for which humanity had no herd immunity, no vaccination or proven treatment and about which it had scant medical knowledge.[7] During the three weeks of delay in declaring a new virus, millions of airline passengers boarded planes in Wuhan and flew to foreign airports around the world, and the virus was spread to dozens of countries, infecting thousands of people (Cyranoski 2020). By February 20, more than 74,000 people in 34 provinces in China were infected and more than 200 people had died.[8] During those same weeks, passengers from around the world also arrived in Wuhan, became infected and carried the virus unwittingly around China and then brought it home to their families, friends and communities in 26 other countries. Within a month of the declaration of the novel coronavirus, the World Health Organisation established a Global Surveillance System and reported that the virus had infected people around the world including hundreds of people on cruise ships that incubated the virus among the closely packed passengers as they travelled.[9] Governments closed their borders, grounded aeroplane fleets and isolated their populations to reduce transmission of the virus. Investigative journalists worked to gather, to verify and to write articles to provide people with timely, accurate health information; to convey medical advice; to convey the many changes in government regulations and a raft of other information as new issues arose. Journalists alerted people to the new disease threat, the need for isolation to slow the spread of the virus and tracked the public health response and focused public attention on the need for medical staff to have adequate protective equipment. The complex reporting was carried out under trying conditions and sometimes while reporters themselves were in isolation.

News coverage resulting from investigative journalism work often takes many years to emerge in the public arena, and even longer for the revelations contained in the media coverage to be addressed by the authorities. Two investigative journalists who feature in this book first met a particular whistleblower in 2008. Their initial investigation spanned several countries, took eight months to complete and was published in 2011. The allegations were investigated by police and the offenders were finally convicted in 2018. This 10-year time frame required the reporters to build and maintain rapport and trust with their contacts over many years, to spend time following up leads that may not always result in stories and to risk and fight legal challenges to publication. Despite these challenges, the importance and significance of the work should be recognised. The news coverage resulted in police investigations being launched that had previously been refused. The offending company was ordered to pay fines totalling $21million. Several staff were convicted of criminal offences including conspiracy to commit foreign bribery in three different countries. The personal risks to reporters of undertaking investigative journalism as a career must also be considered. These two reporters were both subpoenaed to give evidence in court about the identity of their confidential source.[10] Investigative journalism is not for the faint-hearted, but it is necessary for the maintenance of healthy democratic societies.

Media coverage resulting from major investigative journalism projects frequently drives the public news agenda and sometimes the legislative agenda of governments as well, when parliaments respond to the need for change as articulated via the media, backed by public awareness and public opinion. Without investigative journalism, democratic societies do not have a watchdog – a fourth estate – reporting on the activity of the three estates of government: the Parliament, the Executive and the

Courts. The fourth estate role of the media in democratic societies can be seen in the five functions of communication media in democratic societies: to inform citizens, to educate citizens, to provide a platform for political discourse, to report on government activity and to provide a platform for varying political viewpoints to be expressed (McNair 2003). Media coverage produced with the guidance of ethical precepts provides reliable information for citizens which informs their daily activities and choices. A variety of political perspectives allows citizens to consider various policy options, informing their political choices at elections. This book focuses on the huge investigative potential for reporters in hyperconnected societies to be able to find and report on issues and topics that would have previously been almost impossible or impractical to carry out. The timing of these stories is far longer than the daily 24/7 news cycle, far longer than the weekly political cycle and far longer, at times, than the annual financial cycle. Many of these stories take time to patiently uncover and it then may take years to expose the true intentions, bring criminals to justice, expose the extent of corruption and yield the necessary legislative change.

Important questions are now being raised amongst media scholars about the future of journalism – and particularly the costly and time-consuming practice of investigative journalism such as the story of Dr Li – and whether our societies can afford *not* to have investigative journalism. This question is being asked because the business model that has supported journalism financially from advertising revenues for the past few hundred years is no longer viable (Hamilton 2016). In addition the pandemic has led to a media extinction event in which 17 per cent of surveyed media organisations reported revenue falling by more than 75 per cent in the first three months of the pandemic (Posetti, Bell and Brown 2020). The question we must answer is: What if there had been no journalist to see, and verify and republish Dr Li's post and letter, and to publish them widely enough for the world beyond China to realise that a global pandemic was on the way? I argue in this book that investigative journalism is necessary. It is my intention to encourage, inspire and enable anyone who wishes to embark upon or to continue a career in investigative journalism. Currently there are major difficulties to be overcome including the lack of funding available for the work due to digital disruption. However, I argue that the threats caused by digital technology have also produced new opportunities for investigative journalists to undertake the work faster and more cost-effectively whilst maintaining sound ethical practices, and to look for a variety of income streams from their work including writing books, creating oral history archives and making documentaries or podcasts.

The challenges presented by digital disruption of previous analogue business models are far-reaching. Press barons who monopolised the power of the printing press have substantially lost that monopoly. Digital disruption means that anyone with an internet connection can now communicate with anyone else on earth almost instantaneously for little or no cost – everyone has a virtual printing press. Additionally, information has suddenly been democratised as search engines enable internet-connected devices to search for information very quickly and easily using common language search terms. The storage of news coverage that is readily available creates enduring networks of digital connection between the information and anyone who is interested in that information. Many media outlets have tried to maintain their business model by creating paywalls to their content but that has the downside risk of reducing their readership and therefore the price they can demand for advertising space. No easy solutions have yet appeared. For young people considering career options, the number of reporters who have been made redundant means there are relatively few jobs available. For reporters who have been made redundant, it may be difficult to find alternative work. Journalism schools around the world are downsizing and some are closing or merging with others. All these challenges make journalism a brave choice of career for those determined to find a job in the industry and to succeed in it.

However, digital disruption also has some important upsides. Communication technologies now make collaboration easier than ever before. That collaboration may be a so-called micro-collaboration where as few as two or three reporters work together within one office, or in separate offices in different states or countries to investigate an issue and publish in one or more publications in one or more states or countries (Gearing and Berglez 2019). Collaborations may also include hundreds of reporters all working together, sharing vast caches of documents and data and publishing simultaneously in dozens or even hundreds of publications in many countries on an agreed date. The International Consortium of Investigative Journalists (ICIJ) has produced global coverage that has led over several years to significant global governmental responses including collective legislative change, especially in the area of tax avoidance (Berglez and Gearing 2018). So, ironically, at a time when the industry and journalists are facing their toughest working conditions, they are more needed than ever and have the best possible tools to do the most exciting and necessary and powerful work as a nascent global fourth estate. This global fourth estate is an extension of the fourth estate role played by investigative journalism within individual countries. The emerging *global* fourth estate is making it possible for the global community to respond to diverse but pressing global risks and threats – such as money laundering and tax evasion, climate change and the global pandemic. The term global investigative journalism, introduced in this book, is the action of a journalist or journalists to investigate and report on issues that call powerful individuals, corporations or governments to account in their home country, or in a foreign country or countries. This is achieved by means of investigative journalism that relies on social media platforms and Web based communication technologies that enable journalists and media outlets to form networks of collaboration across national boundaries and time zones. I argue that global investigative journalism is needed, and that the technological means are now available. This book springs from my hope that journalism students and reporters will find inspiration in the case studies in this book and be ready to seize the day when opportunities arise.

Collaboration can result in faster, far more cost-effective investigations that yield powerful news coverage that focuses the public spotlight on issues that need to be addressed. When local, state or national authorities such as police, governments, businesses, organisations or politicians fail, journalism can call them to account in the public arena. Reporters who are able to marshal incontrovertible evidence and convincing whistle-blowers can publish news coverage that brings public opinion to bear, forcing reluctant authorities to take action. Injustices can be repaired, corruption can be exposed and expunged, outdated laws can be scrapped, criminals can be apprehended and placed on trial. In all the cases in this book, people silenced by circumstances were able to find their voice and speak truth to power. In the case of Dr Li, the truth escaped via social media into the mainstream media, enabling health officials around the world to respond. Dr Li's trail of online data and metadata enabled reporters to verify what happened and when. Journalists were able to translate and track Dr Li's social media posts and piece together his extraordinary medical discovery and, importantly, the quick and deadly progress of his illness, sparing many other people a similar demise.

The crisis

In the early 2000s social media platforms enabled billions of people who were already connected to the World Wide Web to be electronically connected to each other. As staggering as these changes were, they spelled seeming disaster for investigative journalism. Media companies that had used advertising revenue to fund journalism slashed their budgets and sacked thousands of reporters who were working for newspapers, radio and television news outlets. Businesses that once had to pay for advertising space to reach their customers could now communicate electronically with customers and potential customers online and advertise online for a fraction of the cost. It seemed like investigative journalism was dying; but in places, there were the first signs of a rebirth occurring in which some reporters were using the new technology and new techniques to enable them to report on stories anywhere in the world. So, while there is a funding crisis, there are also opportunities to save time, money and travel by using the new tools available in the nascent practice of global investigative journalism in the network society.

Media companies were generally reluctant and slow to engage with the internet for a combination of reasons. First, journalists realised that new technologies were an unnecessary part of their newsgathering methods because they already had wide networks of reliable contacts (Moon and Hadley 2014). Secondly, new technologies were perceived as a threat because media companies did not want to believe the internet could steal the so-called rivers of gold from classified advertising upon which their profitability relied (Spyridou et al. 2013; Nicholas et al. 1998; Berglez 2013). Thirdly, given falling revenues, new technologies were considered too costly to embrace (Rosenthal 2011). Consequently, advertising revenue dried up suddenly, and tens of thousands of reporters who had covered local, state, national and international news became redundant. Media empires that had used advertising revenues from geographic areas to subsidise publication of news to those areas were suddenly outperformed by global online advertising platforms. The business model that had supported news production became obsolete and there was no viable alternative means to financially support the news industry.

The contraction in the journalism labour force during the 2000s went largely unheralded, often by the very media organisations that were most affected. Mass sackings of reporters, sub-editors and associated newspaper staff occurred as advertising budgets suddenly moved to online platforms. So sudden and severe was the contraction in newspaper readership that media commentators and academics forecast the "end of newspapers" (McChesney and Pickard 2011). US media academics Robert McChesney and Victor Pickard co-edited a collection of essays about the coming doom, including *Will the Last Reporter Please Turn Out the Lights: The Collapse of Journalism and What can be Done to Fix It* (McChesney and Pickard 2011).

Two events galvanised my interest in the potential opportunities offered by digital investigative tools and digital news gathering and reporting. First, a flash flood disaster in 2011 in Toowomba, my home city, that quickly became world news alerted me to the hyperconnectivity of individuals in the digital society. Secondly, an approach by a whistleblower in the UK in 2012, asking me to investigate a story in England and to publish the story there, helped me to realise the global nature of connections between potential news sources and reporters.

The suddenness and revolutionary nature of the changes to reporting techniques during the flash flood prompted me to engage in a research master's degree to examine what could be learned about reporting on disasters in the digital age using digital technologies and techniques. While reporting on the flood and its aftermath for a year, I upgraded my old analogue audio skills to digital and made a radio documentary. I transcribed the recorded interviews with survivors and rescuers and used them as the basis for a book about the disaster (Gearing 2012b). The children who were affected by the flood can hear the voices of these rescuers and flood survivors in dozens of recorded interviews that now form part of Queensland state library's archive of the disaster (Gearing 2012a). My motivation for writing the book was that very young children who were bereaved of their parents in the flood would one day have questions about what happened. The children deserved thorough answers and I saw this as the role of the reporter. I came to realise that the role of the investigative journalist can be extended from reporter to researcher, historian and investigator as they document the people, events and places at a time of extraordinary trauma, upheaval and change (Gearing 2013a). Many socio-political changes were made in the flood-affected communities, partly due to news coverage about what happened to people during the disaster. One community was shifted to higher ground; mobile phone coverage was improved; warning systems were installed; isolated river gauges were networked; and helicopter swift water rescue methods and equipment were adapted and upgraded. Some of my research led to a government inquiry into the onset of the flood in the worst-hit town of Grantham (Sofronoff 2015). Five years after the flood, I returned to document the recovery of the people and communities in the flood zone in order to update the book and to write a research article making recommendations to better scaffold the recovery of survivors in the years after a disaster (Gearing 2017, 2018). The willingness of disaster survivors to speak to reporters was surprising given the severity of the disaster. This led to further research on why disaster survivors speak to reporters and producing guidelines for reporters preparing to report on various types of disasters in the digital age (Gearing 2013b, 2019).

The second event that galvanised my interest in the potential of digital news gathering landed as an email request from an unknown person in the UK in late 2012. Eli Ward disclosed child sexual abuse by a very senior cleric in England – a cleric who had worked in Australia at a school that I had written about in an article some four years earlier, in 2009. My article covered a subsequent school principal, also a priest, who had been jailed for child sex offences and who had also been appointed to very senior roles in the Australian Church.[11] I had already written hundreds of articles about the scandal of institutional sexual abuse of children, beginning in 2001 when I reported on a landmark civil action when the first Australian court found that the owner of a school could be found vicariously liable for the sexual assault of a child in the school by a staff member.[12] The Diocese of Brisbane owned the school and the Archbishop of the Diocese had become the Governor-General of Australia a few months before the trial. He resigned after the findings of an inquiry were released in 2003.[13]

My initial response to Eli Ward expressed sympathy with his plight as a victim of child sexual assault. However, I believed at the time that it would be impossible to investigate and publish a story overseas. Then, after meeting Mr Ward in Cambridge while I was in the UK, I promised to follow up some leads back in Australia. The discovery of another victim – in Australia – of the same offender opened the way for an international investigation that led to an inquiry in the UK and a review of the seal of the confessional that had enabled the offender to escape prosecution. It became clear that undertaking the investigation from regional Queensland was not only possible but easily manageable, relatively fast and inexpensive. I collaborated with senior reporters in Australia and England, and together we published the revelations of the coverup of the paedophile Dean of Manchester, Robert Waddington on the front pages of national newspapers in two different countries simultaneously in May 2013 in their first-ever collaborative publication.

The effect of the two projects in bringing justice for the victims and socio-political change piqued my interest about which kinds of digital tools and techniques other reporters might be using in Australia, especially in capital city newspapers. This book mainly comprises my PhD research findings in the form of narrative accounts by leading journalists about how they found, verified and published news coverage that resulted in them being selected as a finalist or that won Australia's highest industry awards for investigative journalism in 2013 in the annual Walkley Awards. Interestingly, the changes and the criminal proceedings triggered by those stories have only recently been finalised, emphasising the long timeframe over which investigative journalism projects can run. The Awards select the best journalism produced in the preceding year based on the criteria of ethics, newsworthiness, public benefit, originality, research, impact, writing, creative flair, inclusiveness, innovation and production. Fortunately, the reporters I interviewed willingly shared their experiments, ideas and techniques for digital connectivity. Despite being based in Australia, they were reporting from different locations including the UK, Europe, the US, Israel, India, Bangladesh, Indonesia and West Papua.

The great disruption

The changes to how people connect with each other and with journalists during natural disasters were very sudden. As the flash flood struck Toowoomba – a city 700m above sea level – terrestrial phone lines and mobile towers were destroyed or overloaded. Apart from Citizen's Band radios, communication was possible only via the World Wide Web using email or social media. Residents immediately flocked to social media platforms, seeking and sharing information, reporting people missing or dead and giving warnings to downstream communities. Local legacy media – newspaper, radio and television – were outpaced in their newsgathering ability by a community Facebook page in Toowoomba created by freelance journalist Susannah Birch.[14] Within 24 hours the page had a global following of 37,000 people – far exceeding the readership of the local newspaper. Suddenly the community was in conversation: sharing eyewitness accounts, giving warnings, verifying and responding to information faster than newspapers, radio or television outlets could manage. Relatives and friends of people in the disaster zone who could not make contact used the page to check on the welfare of family members and friends.

Within hours of striking the city of Toowoomba, the "inland tsunami" became global news. Video footage uploaded to YouTube was broadcast around the world. What was striking about the flood was that not only were media outlets hobbled by the loss of analogue communications, emergency services were too. Police were unable to verify missing or dead people; but journalists who lived locally and who had social network contacts could confirm deaths and report them on the day of the disaster. Police identification of bodies took several weeks in some cases. Police also turned to the media for public information about missing people. Several people thought to have died were able to be confirmed alive within a couple of days.[15] Social media platforms made it possible for local residents and investigative reporters to collaborate quickly to verify that specific people spotted in flood waters had survived.[16] Reporting methods developed over 30 years were suddenly superseded. Social media platforms had created an online forum between reporters and their communities in which information and questions flowed quickly in both directions. Information could be verified almost instantly by the crowd. Groups could be formed online that were exclusive, to gather and hold information. Other groups could be public to give and receive information that did not need to be exclusive. News communication became a two-way conversation with the affected community rather than a one-way discourse from authorities, via reporters, to residents.

It was not until 2012 that I began to understand the global scope of this digital disruption. I was in Europe when I received an email from a person in England asking me to report on a story that had been rejected by his local newspaper and a national newspaper in England. Soon after meeting him I had to return to Australia. Once home, I spent six months interviewing and researching the story. I formed a collaboration with a political editor at *The Australian* and the crimes editor at *The Times* in London. A joint publication day was brokered, and the story ran on the front page of both national newspapers on the same day. The revelations led to an inquiry in the UK. As a result of the coverage and the inquiry, the whistleblowers were vindicated. The Anglican Church was proved to have protected a serial child sex offender who had been shipped to Australia in 1953, returned to the UK and eventually been promoted until he was appointed Dean of Manchester where he continued offending against children (Cahill 2014). A story that had existed since the 1960s became front-page national news in 2013 when the corruption was finally exposed.

In late 2016 I received another important story lead, this time about the cover-up of decades of child sexual abuse by a monk at a Catholic monastery in Wales. This time I wrote for the *Guardian* because the masthead had a presence in Australia and in the UK, making the collaboration in-house rather than between different media organisations. Once the story was published, I was invited to collaborate with BBC Radio Wales. That investigation led to calls for an inquiry by the Welsh Government and for a case study by the Independent Inquiry into Child Sexual Abuse in the UK.

It is now clear that the same online and social media tools that work locally, also work internationally and globally. They work across time zones, they jump state and national borders without passports, tickets or plane travel. Webcams enable face-to-face online interviews between reporters and news sources despite the geographic distance between them. Articles, audio and video can be delivered almost instantaneously via email to any media organisation on the globe. This book will show how individual reporters can undertake global investigative journalism in the emerging network society, from finding leads and news sources locally or internationally, using the power of the Web tools available via social media and Web based communications. Recognising that investigative journalism is under threat is reason enough to try new approaches because to give up without trying would be to devalue a profession that has contributed to the rise of democracy in the free world over centuries. Many journalist-authors since Bernstein and Woodward have written or edited books about the importance of investigative journalism in the past and the new techniques being used (Bernstein and Woodward 1974; Lashmar 2020; Pilger 2011; Hamilton 2016; Leigh 2019). Among the reporters I interviewed in my primary research was Richard Baker, who acknowledged the current crisis, but continues in his work because he believes that simply giving up is not an option while ever there is a way forward. Richard Baker says, "you've got to find a way to give [investigative journalism] a presence – to back it" whilst recognising the financial challenges. Quotations from Richard Baker and the other research participants are attributed by name in this text but without repetitive formal referencing.

Quality news outlets still value investigative journalism and continue to fund high-cost investigative journalism despite the severe budget cuts they are making to general reporting budgets due to digitisation. Journalism foundations such as the Walkley Foundation run annual awards which media outlets and reporters compete to win every year. Major news outlets still have investigative teams producing substantial exclusive stories every three or four months which cut through the news noise of the 24/7 news cycle. Stories that win awards also boost the profile of the media outlet amongst potential advertisers.

Dramatic rebirth

The loss of known services, such as reliable daily news bulletins or news coverage that exposes corruption, is difficult to conceptualise until it happens. The closure of thousands of newspapers around the world over the past decade and the sudden closure of thousands more as a result of the SARS-CoV-2 pandemic has focused the attention of the public on the need for incisive, ethical, investigative reporting to understand current events that might be life or economically endangering. The public has seen how leaders in other countries have responded (or failed to respond) to the risk of SARS-CoV-2 as a medical and economic threat to their country and people. This life-sized experiment has allowed citizens, and even children, to see clearly the need for a free press, the need for checks and balances on power and the need for whistleblowers to be able to signal danger or corruption via the media. More than 60 per cent of journalists in a survey in May 2020 reported feeling a greater commitment to journalism, an increase in reader trust and higher audience engagement (Posetti et al. 2020). Paradoxically, journalists have experienced positive personal growth despite the enormous financial and psychological pressures of their work during the pandemic.

Whether there will be a dramatic rebirth of investigative journalism or not will depend on many factors. One of these factors is the academy and their current journalism students who may want to become investigative reporters. Reporters themselves acknowledge the difficulties of an increased speed of work in the 24/7 news cycle but they remain dedicated to the fundamentals of analogue news-gathering methods: undertaking face-to-face interviews, shoe leather journalism, building trust with news contacts, making and maintaining news contacts and relying on documentary evidence with the aim of placing social issues on the public agenda for attention and resolution in service of democracy. The emergence of several international networks of investigative journalists indicates this process is beginning. ICIJ director Gerard Ryle is optimistic that "the same technology that is destroying our industry has the power to rebuild it" by courting and seeking to protect whistleblowers, by collecting data and by establishing teams of investigative reporters. Gerard Ryle believes that far from journalism dying, the profession has the potential to enter a new 'golden age' (Ryle 2013). Cross-border collaborative journalism is a relatively young phenomenon and there is little scholarship available so far (Alfter and Candea 2019). In practice, however, cross-border collaborative journalism has proved powerful. Alfter and Candea believe a deeper understanding is needed between practitioners and researchers of new approaches that are being used.

One of Australia's most acclaimed investigative journalists, Richard Baker, sees his role as 'changing things and helping people' who report on a system that is failing people, or ignoring people, to expose it and see changes made to repair the problems.

> That, for me, is why our job is important. Otherwise it is just disposable stuff – and I do not want to be a journalist who just writes click-bait. I would just do something else – get paid better and do something else.

The importance of the work is underlined by the findings of an Australian Defence Force inquiry that revealed in November 2020 that special forces soldiers allegedly unlawfully killed civilians during the Afghan War (Gaynor 2020). Australian Broadcasting Corporation (ABC) reporter Mark Willacy won a Gold Walkley Award for his investigation that aired helmet cam footage of an Australian soldier shooting an unarmed man in a wheat field who was holding prayer beads, in the first known war crime captured on a video camera.[17] The Prime Minister has signalled that the culture of the Australian Defence Force would be transformed as a result of the report findings.[18]

To be reborn, investigative journalism needs the public – a well informed and politically interested public – a public willing to fund ethical, incisive, investigative journalism. Journalists rely heavily on members of the public who collect information and evidence – sometimes for many years – and blow the whistle, providing the basis for an investigation that has the potential to raise community awareness, change government policy or expose corruption. Functional democracies are not free from problems but they have a recognised, orderly and peaceful means for problems to be placed in the 'market square' for discussion and resolution. This is an indication of success rather than failure.

Secondly, investigative journalism needs whistleblowers. These individuals and groups of people have special access to, or possession of, knowledge that makes them simultaneously powerful and vulnerable. They have the power to speak the knowledge and to have issues addressed, but they also risk being punished, losing their job, losing sleep, freedom and sometimes their lives by speaking about what they know. Anyone considering being a whistleblower will find information in this book about how ethical, highly skilled reporters work; the efforts they go to to protect whistleblowers; and the protection and care that can be put in place to provide the best possible degree of safety. There are upsides to being a whistleblower in terms of catharsis. Knowing about issues or corruption but not being able to speak about them or to have them resolved can have a long-term emotional and psychological downside. Speaking the truth can lead to a catharsis and empowerment of the whistleblower – although this cannot be guaranteed.

In the digital society, there are far more opportunities for whistleblowers to divulge information anonymously. Digital connection and networks also enable whistleblowers to select and contact specialist reporters anywhere in the world. In the cohort of shortlisted and award-winning journalists reported in my 2016 study, half of the shortlisted stories came from sources who were completely unknown to the reporter. In these cases, it was the whistleblower who chose and sought out a reporter with experience in writing stories on similar topics or stories of similar complexity or gravity, or who worked for a trusted mainstream media masthead. In some cases the whistleblower chose a local reporter, in other cases a reporter who was interstate or overseas. Richard Baker described the effort he goes to to protect his sources.

> [Contacts] require you to protect their confidentiality because they might not be allowed to talk. Their employment contracts forbid them from doing so. So, it is really important that we do what we can to respect that. And that adds a degree of challenge to doing that work because it is not hard to triangulate on mobile phone calls or emails and identify the source of the leak. So being aware of that, we have got to arrange other methods of communication — and that takes a lot of time and energy and adds to the complexity of the job.

Despite the digital tools now available, a dramatic rebirth of investigative journalism is not guaranteed. Funding is very tight, personnel are stretched. But there are ways forward. My hope is, of course, that there will be a dramatic rebirth of investigative journalism. There are already indications that reporters are adopting digital tools, discovering their power and continuing to experiment. Most of the reporters in this text who won national acclaim for their reporting have subsequently won further awards. This is an indication that early adopters of new technologies or methods continue to produce media coverage that their industry peers hold up as best practice.

Behind the scenes

This book gives readers a behind-the-scenes look at how investigative journalism was suddenly changed and empowered by the digital disruption that threatened to destroy it. Leading reporters share here their trepidation about using digital tools, the discovery of their power and the changes wrought by the coverage they produced. A young female reporter in Sydney, for example, tells how she was distressed by the calamity of the collapse of a clothing factory in Bangladesh in 2013. The factory owners employed people for minimal wages working in a poorly built factory. How could she report on this human-made disaster from Australia and effect change in another country? Her investigation succeeded in calling business and government to account and contributed to fairer wage agreements for workers and better building standards in Bangladesh. Another reporter had been hearing disclosures of horrific child sexual abuse for years. Her reporting sparked a Royal Commission that has triggered further inquiries overseas that have led to new laws being enacted to help keep children safe.

Investigative reporters rarely share their secrets. This book has been made possible by the generosity of the reporters involved who were willing to discuss their creative use of digital technologies in the interests of giving new generations of reporters ideas for continuing the proud traditions of investigative journalism to guard democracy, to give voice to the voiceless in society and to be change agents in society. My early experiments, and those of my reporter colleagues who participated in my research, show that traditional journalistic skills remain vital but the digital tools enable silenced news sources to speak, allow stories to be told that may have been concealed for many years and drive community change, and change in the state, national and even global arena. Some journalists interviewed in this research are beginning to embrace digital technologies, but they are primarily self-taught. They are experimenting and discovering what works in various situations and what is risky or simply doesn't work. Almost all the reporters were reluctant or very reluctant to engage with new technologies; some were frightened of the possible negative consequences, some were nervous of stepping into the unknown. A few are keen and adept. The research indicates that the savings in time, travel and finances that are possible because of digitisation are enough to enable investigative journalism to continue and to call the powerful to account in various ways. So great is our reliance now on digital connection to practise investigative journalism that one of the main downside risks for reporters and media outlets is *disconnection* from the internet.

A well-informed and engaged citizenry is vital to the proper functioning of democratic governments. This book is timely because it articulates the methods that have been used to produce ethically sound news coverage that results in socio-political change. With appropriate skills and ideas, journalists will be well placed to face the challenges ahead and to be ready to take opportunities when they arise. The ICIJ has warned that "Broadcast networks and major newspapers have closed foreign bureaus, cut travel budgets and disbanded investigative teams. We are losing our eyes and ears around the world precisely when we need them most" (Keena 2014). While traditional investigative reporting skills remain vitally important, a range of new skills can be used to enhance investigative power and speed while reducing costs, by using social media, Web based communications, as well as individual and organisational collaborations. The examples included here provide an insight into an emerging globalisation of journalism in which investigative journalists are creating coverage which plays a role in highlighting injustice and which acts as a global fourth estate.

Notes

1 Stephanie Hegarty. 2020. "The Chinese doctor who tried to warn others about coronavirus." London, *BBC News*. https://www.bbc.com/news.
2 Ibid.
3 European Centre for Disease Prevention and Control. 2020. "COVID-19 situation update worldwide." https://www.ecdc.europa.eu/en/geographical-distribution-2019-ncov-cases
4 *BBC News*. 2020. "Coronavirus declared global health emergency by WHO." 31 January 2020. https://www.bbc.com/news/world-51318246.
5 *BBC News*. 2020. "Coronavirus declared global health emergency by WHO." 31 January 2020. https://www.bbc.com/news/world-51318246.
6 Evelyn Cheng. 2020. "Contactless delivery, online grocery shopping and other ways home-bound Chinese are trying to get food and stay safe." Beijing, *CNBC*. 6 February 2020. https://www.cnbc.com/2020/02/07/virus-out break- forces-chinese-to-stay-at-home-and-order-more-delivery.html.

7 Kok Xinghui. 2020. "Singapore closes borders to all foreign travellers from China to stem spread of coronavirus." This week in Asia. Hong Kong, *South China Morning Post*. https://www.scmp.com/week-asia/health-envir onment/article/3048441/singapore-closes-borders-all-chinese-travellers-stem.
8 World Health Organisation. 2020. "Coronavirus disease 2019 (COVID-19): Situation Report 31." 20 February 2020. https://www.who.int/docs/default-source/coronaviruse/situation-reports/20200220-sitrep-31-covid-19.pdf.
9 Ibid.
10 Paul Anderson. 2013. "Fairfax reporters Nick McKenzie and Richard Baker ordered to give evidence in banknote case." *HeraldSun*. 25 January 2013. https://www.heraldsun.com.au/news/law-order/fairfax-reporters-nick-mckenzie-and-richard-baker-ordered-to-give-evidence-in-banknote/news-story/7e6020e5862b557ad5aa3cd9300e5568?sv=9608f7f653d4a77f783ac6e9d4e698df.
11 Amanda Gearing. "Archbishop's chaplain behind bars at last." On Line Opinion: Australia's e-journal of social and political debate. 29 April 2009.
12 Amanda Gearing. 2012. "Suffer the children." *The Courier-Mail*. 15 December 2001.
13 "Hollingworth quits." 2003. *The Age*. 26 May 2003.. https://www.theage.com.au/national/hollingworth-quits-20030526-gdvrnh.html.
14 S. Birch. 2011. "Toowoomba & Darling Downs flood photos & info [Online]." This site has been archived.
15 Amanda Gearing and H. Thomas. 2011. "The seconds that separated life and death." *The Australian*. 12 January 2011.
16 Amanda Gearing and Sarah Elks. 2011. "Toowoomba's 'miracle girl' surfaces." *The Australian*. 20 January 2011. www.theaustralian.com.au.
17 Mark Willacy. 2020. "Inside *ABC Investigations*' 14-month probe into alleged war crimes by Australian soldiers in Afghanistan." *ABC Investigations*. 20 November 2020.
18 *BBC News*. 2020. "Australia may prosecute soldiers over Afghanistan 'war crimes.'" 12 November 2020. https://www.bbc.com/news/world-australia-54912722.

2 Reconceptualising investigative journalism

Eli Ward was watching television in 2012 when he saw a news bulletin alleging British comedian Jimmy Savile had been a prolific child sex offender. Details in the stories of Savile living a double life – associating with royalty but also sexually abusing children – exploded in his mind. Eli Ward realised at that moment that Robert Waddington, the Dean of Manchester, whom he had seen as a friend was actually a child sex offender. Ward was staggered by the depth of the betrayal of his childhood innocence. Memories of his childhood came flooding back, playing and replaying in his mind. Ward reported the offences to the police in 2012, some 30 years after he had been abused. He also wrote to the Archbishop of Canterbury to report the offences to the Church. Feeling a strong compulsion to expose the offending and also the corruption of the Church in protecting the offender, Ward spoke to reporters at his local newspaper and a national newspaper but they did not publish the story. Ward was struggling psychologically, and he had no pattern for survival as a victim of child sexual abuse. The only other victim of Waddington who Ward knew about had died by suicide (Cahill 2014). Ward thought he was the only victim. But was he? He went to his computer and typed in key words: 'Waddington,' 'priest,' 'paedophile.' Ward knew that Waddington had lived for many years in Australia and expanded his search by adding the names of the two boarding schools where Waddington had worked: The Slade School in Warwick and St Barnabas School in Ravenshoe, both Anglican schools in Queensland. To his surprise, Ward found an article written in 2009 naming a subsequent headteacher of St Barnabas School as a paedophile priest who had just been jailed. He searched the author's name and found her email address, sent an email and hoped the reporter might be able to shed some light on the dark past of Robert Waddington that might reflect some understanding into his own life.

Analogue connections could not have enabled Ward to independently find a specific reporter in another country who had written about a particular school with reference to a particular topic. In addition, analogue

DOI: 10.4324/9781003139980-2

archives within institutions such as Churches that have controlled information flows are private repositories of information that can be concealed from the public. Even if Ward knew other victims of Waddington existed, how would he find them – especially if he had no name? What Ward did not know was that the Church in Australia and the Church in England knew about Waddington's crimes and that there were victims in both countries but they had not admitted it to the victims, leaving them isolated and believing they were the only one making an allegation. In the digital era, the ability to find other victims, to be validated and vindicated is possible. The digital and journalistic revolution is illustrated by Ward's ability to make connections for himself, due to the storage and searchability of online data. So revolutionary is this power that it makes previous theories of the practice of analogue journalism less relevant. Tasks that were once impossible are now possible. The new power is connection – private and public networks of connection – and the power and creativity to imagine and build novel networks.

Network theory

Theories of journalism devised in the pre-digital era when authorities such as governments, businesses and organisations supplied and validated news and information are becoming less useful as descriptors of the process of investigative journalism. New paradigms are needed to better understand the dynamics of a rapidly changing digital age in which communication networks carry information instantaneously, globally, for little or no cost. Theories of journalism that capture the importance and relevance of connection with, or disconnection from, this global network provide the potential to establish a better understanding of the revolutionary changes now occurring in investigative journalism. Network theory, for example, illuminates the quality of connection and disconnection, helping media scholars and reporters to better understand what is happening.

In the case of Eli Ward, digital storage of the news story meant that one article created at a different point in time remained accessible to someone overseas several years later. The news story had, in effect, created a digital network of its own, linking anyone searching for keywords including the name of the school and the topic of child sexual abuse. The age of the story was less important than the *connections* it enabled readers to make. Archiving the past in a searchable format is becoming far more important. Deadlines, scoops and exclusive stories remain important in breaking news but the archiving of the past in accessible formats enables the news itself to create networks that endure long after the original news story has passed (Barnhurst 2013). Instead of the article disappearing within a day of publication, it endured online in a format accessible from anywhere, enabling the scandal of a priest raping children in an isolated boarding school in Australia and the same priest sexually assaulting children in a cathedral in England to be exposed more than 50 years after the initial concealment of the crimes.

Global journalism

Global journalism is a natural consequence of global digital connection. Peter Berglez has observed that "[g]lobal journalism stems from economic, political, cultural, ecological etc. necessity" and is "the natural consequence of increasing connectedness, boundarylessness and mobility in the world: it is the form of journalism needed in times of globalisation" (Berglez 2008, 855). In digital society, reporters are far more likely to work as a team or collaboration, bringing together expertise in different fields, or collaborating across states or countries. Traditional 'lone wolf' investigative reporting in which reporters kept their own contacts, story leads, methods and story ideas to themselves is gradually being replaced by collaborations of different types at different times. Contact books are not obsolete but they function in a different way in the network society. Contact books are far more likely to be electronically based and to span the country or the globe, as major public sphere issues become more globalised. Topics ranging from climate change to health issues such as the SARS-CoV-2 pandemic are global in nature. Writing about these topics from a national perspective is giving way to a global perspective on how the issues affect global populations and ecosystems.

The balance of power is also shifting away from institutions that collected and held and *withheld* information in favour of individuals who can find and share information and make connections with almost anyone on earth. Institutions that never foresaw the possibility that victims of abuse, for example, may one day be able to find each other and pool their information are suddenly able to be called to account for decades of immoral or illegal behaviour. Similar shifts in power balances have occurred in business, government and other fields of endeavour that will be illustrated in this book. Journalism theories that described how information was gathered from powerful institutions such as government, business and organisational leaders and reported to the masses no longer fit the present digital reality. Castells (2009) asserts that power structures have shifted so radically that the most crucial form of power in the present day is 'network-making' power. This ability also enables those who form networks to programme and re-programme the networks so they favour the interests of those who have formed the network (Castells 2011). Opportunities for investigative journalists to call the powerful to account abound in the network society: reporters can source information from people who were previously isolated and/or silenced; reporters can discover information about powerful people and organisations that was previously withheld (Ryle et al. 2013; Davies 2009), and they can go to the public and 'crowd-source' information using public social media platforms such as Twitter, quickly capturing huge amounts of information that was not previously available. Jesse Abdenour's research indicates that television reporters are using social media to interact with the public, generate story ideas and help produce stories more than other types of reporters (Abdenour 2016). The ability to source information rapidly from a 'crowd,' who may already be engaged watching breaking news via a livestream, has enormous untapped potential.

Social networks

Our understanding of different types of social connections or networks was inspired by the work of internet pioneer Paul Baran. Baran developed his theory of networks during the Cold War to optimise the protection of physical communications networks and to reduce the vulnerability of networks to attack. Communication networks emanating from a central point could be disabled by destroying a single node in the network.

Baran proposed two alternative patterns for physical networks. First, the decentralised pattern in which small numbers of nodes are connected and these in turn are connected to other groups of nodes; and secondly, a distributed pattern in which all nodes are connected to nodes around them creating a 'net' that has no vulnerable central node.

Dominic Boyer (2013) adopted Baran's concept of different patterns of networks to describe patterns of internet-based connection. In Boyer's paradigm, analogue media networks are centralised networks in which information is gathered into a central node and then disseminated to individuals who may have no connection with each other. These unconnected recipient nodes are media consumers such as newspaper readers, television viewers or radio listeners. In contrast, Web based communication networks allow communication between recipients creating a network of hyperconnectivity. These networks are similar in formation to Baran's decentralised or distributed networks in which there are many dissemination points and audience members may be connected with each other and can feed

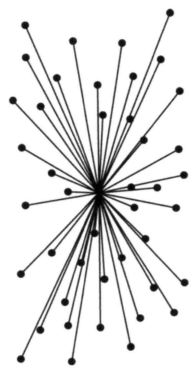

Centralised

Figure 2.1 Paul Baran's centralised network
Source: cited in Boyer 2013, p.150.

back to the source of information, creating a two-way flow of information. There is some evidence to suggest that mainstream news outlets, including newspapers, remain important nodes in the network society, especially when there are significant news events. Axel Bruns and Jean Burgess (2012) analysed patterns of Twitter traffic during natural disasters and found that online audiences chose mainstream media outlets to obtain timely and trusted information about an unfolding natural disaster. Audiences were also able to connect directly with the source of disaster-related information from the lead disaster agency and the state police service, receiving but also *giving information* to the lead agency.

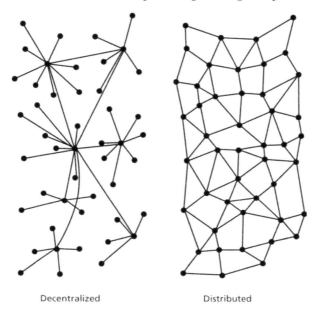

Decentralized   Distributed

Figure 2.2 Paul Baran's decentralised and distributed networks
Source: cited in Boyer 2013, p.150.

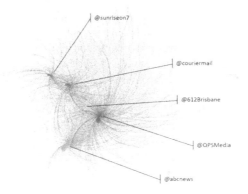

Figure 2.3 Dissemination of tweets for #qldfloods between 10 January and 16
    January 2011
Source: Bruns et al. 2012, 31.

The Queensland Police Service emerged during the disaster as a significant information node providing warnings and information directly to the public via their newly established Facebook page. The importance of the direct-to-the-public disaster information is underlined by the steep rise in audience numbers from fewer than 2,000 before the disaster to more than 160,000 a few days after it. The new digital network connected tens of thousands of people directly with the lead agency and with each other. Castells has observed that social networks have "taken on a new life in our time by becoming information networks, powered by the Internet" allowing many-to-many communication on a global scale (Castells 2001, 1). This transformation offers opportunities but also challenges because the infrastructure of networks can be owned, access to them can be controlled and their uses can be biased (if not monopolised) by commercial, ideological and political interests (Castells 2001, 277). A Cambridge academic, for example, collected personal Facebook data in 2013 to create psychological profiles that could then be sold to political campaigners. The Cambridge Analytica data scandal was exposed in 2018 by a former employee of the company.[1] The shifting power dynamics of global connection present extraordinary opportunities but also have significant risks for democracy in local and national spheres.

The most significant power shift facilitated by global connection is in enabling international and even global accountability. Even in countries where there is not a formal democratic system of government, the global community can speak strongly in the public sphere to recalcitrant governments, in effect bringing the voice of the people, or democracy, to bear. Journalism and democracy have long been twin threads of the same cord. John Milton's famous speech, *Areopagitica,* advocated for a free press to the English Parliament in 1644. He argued that liberty does not guarantee freedom from all grievances, but liberty could be guaranteed by a public forum to freely air complaints and to forge reform. Civil liberty, he said, would be attained "when complaints are freely heard, deeply consider'd and speedily reform'd" (Milton 1644, 1). Over the following four centuries, democratic governments have spread, sweeping aside authoritarian governments across Europe and the Soviet Union (McNair 2009). More recently in the Middle East democratic uprisings have occurred in Egypt, Libya and Yemen during the Arab Spring in 2010–2012. These mass movements are displacing the rule of the rich, the privileged and the powerful with a political order of self-government among equals in which people can "decide for themselves, as equals, how they would live together on earth" (Keane 2010: 3). The implications for politics at a national and even at an international level are little understood.

Investigative journalism

The monitoring of power in democracies by journalists applies to governments and their agencies, but also to businesses, organisations and powerful individuals. Journalists adopt a 'watchdog' role, protecting the interests of the weak, vulnerable, poor and innocent, in the face of decisions and actions by governments, businesses, organisations and institutions which disadvantage the interests of individuals or groups. Although definitions of journalism vary, most theorists include some notion derived from the foundational writings of Walter Lippmann and John Dewey of "public service" (Deuze 2005, 446–447) or "monitoring of power" (Kovach and Rosenstiel 2014). McNair identifies this function as one which goes beyond the role of information gatherer and sharer to one of "critical scrutiny over the powerful, be they in government, business or other influential spheres of society" as part of the fourth estate (McNair 2009, 239). Members of the public are engaging with reporters in far greater numbers, providing information anonymously or as named news sources. This trend is captured by the findings of a survey that reported that audience "involvement and interaction have had the most profound impact on journalists' work." The survey of 605 Australian reporters revealed that 87.2 per cent of respondents said social media, user-generated content, audience feedback and audience involvement in news production had become a lot stronger in the five years to 2013. In addition, another 12.2 per cent of journalists said audience involvement was "somewhat stronger" (Hanusch 2015). The ability of audience members to contact journalists of their choosing in any location and to become involved in issues of relevance to them has the potential to strengthen democracy by giving people a voice in the public sphere and, at times, a collective voice.

The question for Eli Ward was whether the voice of one victim of child abuse could cut through the years of silence and direct public sphere attention to a British institution as powerful as the Church of England? High on Ward's agenda was finding other victims who could validate his experience. High on my agenda was to find other victims (if they existed) to join Ward's voice with any others we could find. As Ward re-interpreted his childhood in light of Waddington being a sex offender, he realised he had important evidence that might help. Ward told me about dozens of framed photos of boys – including him – that were displayed in Waddington's study when he was the Dean of Manchester Cathedral. Further, Ward realised the significance of a new photo added to the collection that he had seen when he visited Waddington some years after the abuse. Ward was determined to try to find this victim and this quest influenced his decision about being anonymous or being named and identified in media coverage. Ward wanted a copy of his childhood photo from Waddington's study published so that the other victim would be able to recognise him from the photos in the study. Ward agreed to be named and photographed as a child and as an adult. Tracking down other victims would also help to verify Ward's allegations. There was a lead in the four eulogies I found online that traced Waddington's career that focused on working with children. The eulogy in *The Times* even ventured that Waddington had "a special gift for teaching boys, which proved useful in his later cathedral appointments when he had responsibility for choristers."[2] Ward found the courage to report the crimes to the Greater Manchester Police. Detectives found a two-page child protection report in the Diocese archives that Ward hoped might unzip the secrets held by the Church about his offender, the 'Reverend' Robert Waddington. The child protection report held a nugget of information – that the Diocese had received "an Australian complaint" about Waddington.[3] No name was given. Would it be possible to find a victim of crime by a specific offender without even having a name? A few years earlier, maybe not. In the digital age? There was every chance. At least the reference in the child protection report to another victim proved that Ward was not alone.

Armed with the evidence of another victim in Australia, I used my laptop while I was still in the UK, to search key words. After a couple of hours, I found a blog post by a person called Bim Atkinson. It read, "My pedophile headteacher and abusive caner was The Most UnReverend Robert Waddington. Some of my other teachers were Brother Peter Gilbert (a Waddington-induced pedophile who is now in gaol)."[4] Here was more evidence that Ward was not alone. I promised to try to find Bim Atkinson once I got back to Australia and – if he was still alive – I would contact him. Waddington's death in 2007 meant Ward would never see Waddington brought to justice but Waddington's death also meant that publication of Waddington's name in connection with child abuse allegations was permissible since defamation was no longer a legal risk. Waddington had died with his public reputation intact. Glowing eulogies were published despite the Church's knowledge that there were victims on both sides of the globe.

Once back in Australia I tracked down Bim Atkinson. He was alive. And he was willing to talk. Surprise contact from a reporter was a shock but Bim felt exhilarated having had a lonely legal battle for 14 years. "I was being vindicated in some sense. I thought 'right, at long last, we've got something, we can do something,'" he told me. Eight

years before Waddington's death, Bim Atkinson had reported Waddington's offences to the Church in England. He was told there were no other
victims. Atkinson also reported it to the police in Australia and an
investigation in 2003 was undertaken but the police would not extradite
Waddington to Australia to face criminal charges. This left Atkinson
without any means of having Waddington brought to justice and left
Atkinson without validation of the sexual offences he suffered from 1964–
1968 as a young child at boarding school. Atkinson was worried that
Waddington had offended against more children after he returned to the
UK and had copies of letters he had written to the Dioceses of Manchester and York, asking officials there to ensure that children were protected
from Waddington.[5] Ward was amazed and distressed when the second
victim of abuse was discovered. Overcoming his own isolation proved to
be a comfort but also increased his anger towards both Waddington and
the Church institution, and increased his determination to seek justice for
Waddington's offences. Ward told me later in an interview about this
dramatic moment:

> I remember the sensation of me receiving that news, which was sad
> obviously but happy that I wasn't alone. After hearing the news I'd
> broken down in tears. It really hit home then that [Waddington]
> was nothing like a friend in any way. Nothing he did was to
> improve my life in any way. It was only to take advantage of me.

Mastery of technology

Castells has observed that the mastery of technology in each period of
history largely determines which societies prosper. He observed that

> The ability or inability of societies to master technology, and parti-
> cularly technologies that are strategically decisive in each historical
> period, largely shapes their destiny, to the point where we could say
> that while technology *per se* does not determine historical evolution
> and social change, technology (or lack of it) embodies the capacity of
> societies to transform.

(Castells 1996, 7)

His observation could apply equally well to the field of journalism. The
following five chapters each begin with a section on my investigation in
England, followed by case studies of other investigations that used
similar techniques or technologies. The reporters who have shared their
methods have done so from an abundance of generosity to assist other

journalists to join them in the work of being an active and viable fourth estate locally, nationally and, at times, globally. Their work was shortlisted or won sections in Australia's national journalism awards for social equity journalism, multimedia-storytelling, coverage of community and regional affairs, scoop of the year, coverage of a major event or issue, business journalism, international journalism and investigative journalism.

Notes

1 Emma Graham-Harrison and Carole Cadwalladr. 2018. "Revealed: 50 million Facebook profiles harvested for Cambridge Analytica in major data breach." London, Guardian Media Group: *The Guardian*. 18 March, 2018.
2 *The Times*. 2007. "The Very Reverend Robert Waddington." London, News UK. 23 March 2007.
3 Diocese of Manchester Child Protection Officer. 2003. Diocese of Manchester Child Protection: Anglican Diocese of Manchester.
4 Bim Atkinson. n.d. "Memories from St Barnabas Boarding School, Ravenshoe Nth Qld …." Old Friends. www.oldfriends.co.nz.
5 M. McKenna, A. Gearing and S. O'Neill. 2013. "Child sex scandal in two countries rocks Anglican Church." Brisbane, NewsCorp: *The Australian*. 10 May 2013. https://eprints.qut.edu.au/68630.

3 Enduring journalism skills and the internet

The arrival of the internet does not equate with the obsolescence of basic journalistic processes such as validating source identities, establishing source credibility and verifying information. In the case of the story in England that I was working on in 2013, this process was conducted slowly because the news sources were dealing with material that was traumatic in nature. In the months after meeting Eli Ward and making contact with Bim Atkinson, the man who had made 'the Australian complaint,' both men gradually located and sent written evidence to me via email, Skype and a secret Facebook group limited to the three of us. Bim Atkinson had hundreds of public and private records including police statements and legal documents amassed over 14 years of civil litigation, and artifacts of his schooling such as class photographs and school publications. The two men were not directly in touch with each other at first because both were emotionally fragile, but as they became more robust they 'met' in a three-way Skype conversation with me. In this first Skype conference call, Eli Ward questioned Bim Atkinson about the play *Peer Gynt* that Waddington had spoken about to him in Manchester. Waddington had taken a group of boys on tour performing the play. Atkinson had kept a copy of the programme that included photographs of the actors. I emailed the programme to Eli Ward, who immediately recognised the children in the programme as those in the framed photos on Waddington's desk in the deanery at Manchester. Bim Atkinson was amazed and enormously encouraged that someone across the globe recognised the photos in a 50-year-old programme for a school play. In a debrief interview about this moment, Bim told me, "It is pretty neat, isn't it, to have somebody recognise the actual kids in the photos and things like that. Yes, it is a little bit spine-tingling." Verification of the sources in this case was necessary for the story, but it had the important side-effect of validating the lived experience of both news sources.

DOI: 10.4324/9781003139980-3

My next level of verification was to test the discreet knowledge of the victims of Waddington as a sex offender. Victims of particular offenders usually become aware of the predator's preference for children with specific physical or personal characteristics, such as hair colour, or children who are highly intelligent or very shy, or who come from a sole parent family. I wanted to find out if Eli Ward could identify a photo of Bim as a child from a group photo of the whole school in Ravenshoe dating from the 1960s when Waddington was the headteacher. I sent the photo to Eli during the Skype conference and asked Eli if he could identify Bim. Ward was immediately able to select Bim from a group of about 40 children. Later Eli explained how he was able to recognise Bim from the photo,

> Robert [Waddington] had photographs of the [victims] all over his study, both in Manchester and in York where he retired and *Peer Gynt* just stood out all the time. I could see straight away that Bim with his white hair was in a photograph on Robert's desk, among others.

This photo recognition and independent verification by a previously unknown person in the UK of 50-year-old school documents kept by Bim Atkinson was a significant factor in persuading me that both men were credible witnesses. I drafted a feature article, verifying the facts from available documents including the newspaper obituaries, police statements, emails, letters, photographs and court documents.[1] A second and third level of verification occurred once the collaboration with the other reporters was formed. Both reporters – one in Queensland and one in London – re-tested the news sources to verify the material to their satisfaction. Both reporters set off to interview the news sources in Australia and England.

On the same day that Michael McKenna flew to North Queensland to interview Bim Atkinson, English reporter Sean O'Neill travelled north from London to interview Eli Ward. Upon meeting both sources and seeing their documentation, both reporters were convinced of the veracity of the victims' claims. Bim Atkinson had grown up on a remote North Queensland cattle station, Gunnawarra, and was sent as a child of nine to St Barnabas Boarding School in Ravenshoe in 1964. It was here that the headteacher, Rev Robert Waddington, and other staff committed repeated serious sex offences against him for the following five years. Bim first reported the offences in 1989 and launched a civil action in 1999 against the Diocese of North Queensland. He also notified the Diocese of York of Waddington's criminality. Both

Dioceses denied the allegations and denied there were any other victims despite knowing of other complaints. They paid Atkinson an ex-gratia compensation payment with no acknowledgement of liability. Across the globe, Eli had been a choir boy in Manchester Cathedral where Dean Robert Waddington groomed and offended against him in the 1980s. His sisters had reported Waddington's offending against Eli and there was the documentary evidence to prove it. The verification carried out by the other two reporters validated my assessment of the credibility of the new sources. Michael McKenna and Sean O'Neill agreed that the international protection of child sex offenders in the Church of England was a very big story.

Michael said:

> Within two weeks we established that the very rudimentary stuff was real and that there was a real story here. Then it came down to investigating, looking at a few ideas that could have taken it further and then realising that we had an absolute ball-tearer of a story.

There was potential for follow up stories and the real possibility that other victims might respond to the coverage.

Digitalisation is not a replacement for analogue investigative skills in making contacts, interviewing, verification and ground-truthing, but rather an augmentation of them. Digital connection is not a replacement for analogue news contacts, but digital connection enhances the size and scope of the networks of connection that reporters can build and maintain. Face-to-face interviews are best practice, and the tyranny of distance can be overcome via various platforms such as Skype and Zoom. Verification of information via documentary evidence is still the foundation of journalistic credibility, and digitisation enables documents to be obtained, stored, shared and transported far more easily and quickly than paper-based documents. Digitisation does not make ground-truthing obsolete. There is no substitute for a reporter being physically present with a person, or at the scene of an event or seeing the aftermath of a disaster in person and being able to describe what they see, hear, touch, taste and smell. So-called 'shoe-leather' journalism is best practice, however digitisation enables reporters to be 'virtually there' via livestreaming technologies that enable audiences to see real-time vision. Despite the power of digitisation, investigative reporters still require high-level analogue interpersonal skills, investigative skills and writing skills.

The four case studies in this chapter reveal the use of highly trained analogue investigative skills. The first investigation, *Dinosaur Stampede,* began as an invitation to an archaeological dig with no guaranteed outcome and became a story that revealed evidence of the world's largest dinosaur stampede. The second investigation, *They're taking our children,* verified that children were being trafficked from West Papua to Indonesia. The third investigation, *Shine the light,* began as a missing person story but grew into the revelation of widespread corruption that eventually sparked a Royal Commission in Australia that precipitated improved child protection in Australia and similar large-scale government inquiries in other countries (Royal Commission into Institutional Responses to Child Sexual Abuse 2017). The fourth investigation, *In my skin,* began as a classroom exercise to enable teenagers to have a voice in their local media which then became part of the national education curriculum. In each case, the story lead was speculative and untested. Each reporter had to spend time working on the idea, verifying the facts and establishing the credibility of the sources and the information.

Case study 1: Dinosaur stampede

Preparation plus opportunity can create success for a particular reporter finding an exclusive story with international significance. The *Sydney Morning Herald* science reporter Nicky Phillips regularly kept in touch with a team of archaeologists. One day in 2013 when she phoned, a team member told her they had found an extensive new dinosaur fossil ground at Riversleigh Station, an isolated cattle property in far North-West Queensland. The team had good form, having discovered three new species of dinosaur a few years earlier.[2] Mrs Phillips asked if she could go with them for their annual dig, and they agreed. The research funding body, *National Geographic*, was not sending a photographer to the dig, so the reporter arranged to take videographer Tony Walters with her to photograph and film the excavation and to film her interviews with the scientists involved, hoping for a find that would be scientifically significant and therefore newsworthy. The dig revealed several new species of dinosaur and the largest known stampede of dinosaurs with at least 3,300 footprints set in stone and dating from 95 million years ago.[3] The reporting crew gathered interviews, still and video vision and sound effects for a planned multimedia digital package including newspaper and online print stories, interactive graphics and video interviews. Once back in Sydney, Nicky Phillips wrote the story and video script and the newspaper's graphic designer, Francisca Sallato, designed interactive graphics to illustrate the story to complement the video footage. Analogue reporting skills were vital to finding this story, securing exclusivity and obtaining still and video vision as the archaeologists revealed the dinosaur stampede. But just as important was the technical team of digital specialists who created artwork and a graphic interface for the multimedia package that lifted the story off the page and screen, attracting the highest possible readership.

Most investigative stories don't have time pressure competition but the discovery of the dinosaur stampede package needed to be produced as quickly as possible to reduce the risk of any other news organisation breaking the story before the multimedia package could be produced. Cooperation between the reporter, the video cameraman, graphic designer, Web designer and the co-ordinator of the overall digital presentation, iPad editor Andrew Forbes, completed the package of stories, photos and graphics as quickly as possible. Andrew Forbes advocated in news conferences for a standout display of the story. Nicky appreciated his role in advocating for the story to be given prominence and his co-ordination of the publication roll-out, enabling her to focus on the writing.

> Andrew acted as the glue and the promoter of the story and the package. Without that advocate in the newsroom for your story, a story can get lost because there are so many reporters doing so many different things. And breaking news is constantly in the background, so editors of different platforms can just be so busy, focused on what's going on at the time that they forget that they've had these reporters out in the field getting this exclusive story that's great and has got all these elements to it.

Andrew Forbes also co-ordinated the staff to make sure the print, images and graphical elements were all ready for release simultaneously.

Nicky Phillips' networking ability in the analogue world was a well-honed skill but her engagement with social media platforms has given her a vastly expanded range of contacts in her science reporting. "More sources mean more opportunities to write about anything and everything, including sensitive and controversial topics," she says. Reporting on science is becoming much more global due to the hyperconnectivity of the internet. When she is chasing a science story, it is as easy to contact someone overseas as it is to contact someone in Australia, or in a home state or town. Nicky Phillips is able to interview contacts overseas before she arrives at work. By the time she arrives at work she may already have done an interview with an overseas scientist.

Award

Nicky Phillips' exclusive coverage of the major fossil find was shortlisted in the national Walkley Awards in 2013 for Multimedia Storytelling in a field of competition that pitched newspaper reporting against radio, television and online competition in the 'All Media' section. For a newspaper article with embedded video footage to win against competing television coverage is testament to the high quality of the work.

Case study 2: *They're taking our children*

Sometimes, analogue newsgathering and production is required because in many countries the internet is patchy or non-existent. The *Sydney Morning Herald* reporter Michael Bachelard was working as the Fairfax correspondent in Indonesia when he heard from an Indonesian contact that children were allegedly being abducted from West Papua and taken to Indonesian Islamic boarding schools to be radicalised. If true, this was an important story. There were substantial challenges to verifying the lead. Lack of internet connections and poor mobile phone signals meant he needed to travel to West Papua to verify the information from people face to face despite the remoteness and danger of travelling to the location. In addition, government restrictions on foreign media workers travelling to West Papua meant he also faced logistical challenges. "West Papua is quite remote – extremely remote – in the areas where this particular thing was happening," he told me.

> People do have mobile phones, but they very often do not work. There is no internet to speak of, no social media. You can try and call people on a mobile phone, but the signal will drop out. It is very hard to hear them. It is a very challenging environment to try and report from remotely, and also obviously, a very challenging environment to get to personally because there are government restrictions on foreign media travelling there.

Bachelard obtained permission from the Indonesian Government to go to West Papua to report on how Australian Government aid money was being spent in West Papua in the fight against AIDS. After obtaining permission, he was able to try to meet the families whose children had allegedly been abducted.

> I made the argument to the Indonesian government that this is Australian government spending, and as an Australian correspondent I should be able to scrutinise what they are doing, and you should give me permission to go to West Papua to do that story.

To his surprise, he obtained permission. He worked on the AIDS funding story by day and the alleged abduction story at night under cover of darkness. "I'd go off and meet these other people about the children's story, and that's really how I managed to stand it up," he said. Bachelard was able to prove that organisations were taking orphaned children or children with single parents from West Papua to Indonesia where they were converted to Islam and radicalised. He said,

> [They] put them in Islamic boarding schools to, in many cases, convert them to Islam. If they are not already Islam … in essence to give them a stronger − we would say more radical − version of Islam for them to be reimported into West Papua which is considered to be a backward, mainly Christian state, by the Islamists in Indonesia.

Award

Michael Bachelard's magazine story "They're taking our children" was published in the weekend news magazine in the *Sydney Morning Herald* and *The Age* and was selected as a finalist in the All Media section for International Journalism in the 2013 Walkley Awards.

Case study 3: *Shine the light*

In 2012, *Newcastle Herald* reporter Joanne McCarthy recognised a name on a police missing person report. She knew the name John Pirona as a victim of child sexual abuse. He had spoken to her some years earlier about the offending by Rev John Denham. Denham had first come to Joanne McCarthy's attention when another victim had phoned her in 2006 to find out why Denham, a child sex offending priest, who had been convicted in 2000, was still working as a priest. For McCarthy, this was a basic fact-checking exercise. The Sydney Court registry told the victim they could find no record of a conviction. Joanne McCarthy asked the victim for a court file number and rang the registry herself. This time, the court staff found the record of conviction. McCarthy had started writing about the convicted paedophile priest and knew that other victims of Denham had committed suicide. When the missing person report was made to the police, she strongly suspected that John Pirona, aged 45, may have done the same. In an interview with me, Joanne explained her initial fears that John was dead and described the connections she had with the family that might enable her to report on the circumstances of his tragic death. "It was obvious that [the police] were only going to find a body. I knew his family. They knew me." Joanne phoned John's wife to ask about John's disappearance.

Joanne McCarthy had become a subject matter expert over the years, knowing the names and career history of many of the offenders, listening to the accounts of hundreds of victims, learning the names of the Church leaders who regularly transferred offenders to different parishes or dioceses and getting to know victim support workers and police. Many of the victims who spoke to her needed emotional and psychological support. She said,

> I had to do a lot of things that went way beyond journalism in terms of really supporting, taking calls from suicidal people and working out a process of how to do that – how to support them – and making sure I had a network of people that I could immediately ring to get help for people who'd just disclosed [abuse].

What they all lacked at the time was access to justice. Police prosecutions were rare. Civil actions were almost impossible. As a consequence, abuse had been rife in trusted institutions that cared for children, destroying the lives of many children.

McCarthy had grown up in the Hunter Valley herself and knew some of the victims and their families. She had heard many harrowing accounts of child sexual abuse and she knew John's predator was a serial offender. She also knew that several Church leaders knew about priests who had been offending for decades but had failed to protect children from them. After years of interacting with Church leaders, McCarthy decided to put questions to Church officials by email rather than in interviews. The Church leaders responded in writing, giving her written evidence of her questions, their answers and the date of their responses. Her database of emails became vitally important in verifying the changes in position of Church officials and instances when officials had contradicted themselves.

When John Pirona went missing, Joanne had already verified a substantial amount of information about Denham. Denham had been offending against boys for at least 18 years, from 1968 to 1986. After his first conviction in 2000, he was subsequently convicted again in 2010 and 2015 for sex offences against 56 boys aged from 5 to 17, making him a serious and prolific offender.[4] Even so, reporting John Pirona's suspected suicide before a body was found was potentially risky. When Joanne obtained John's suicide note, she decided on balance to go ahead but she was very cautious in her approach, balancing the public interest in the story with the right to privacy of a grieving family. In this case, the family was willing to share John's suicide letter, concluding with his message: "Too much pain." Reporting, or not reporting, on suicides is a highly contested area in journalism despite suicide accounting for 800,000 annual deaths globally – a number that is higher than the annual global death toll of war, murder and natural disasters combined (Luce 2019). Guidelines for reporting on suicides were developed as recently as 2019 (Luce 2019).

What began as a missing person story in a regional newspaper grew quickly into a national call for the first extensive and in-depth Royal Commission into institutional responses to child sexual abuse. McCarthy's understanding of the dynamic relationship between journalism and politics meant she saw the tragedy of John's death as a potential turning point for positive change – if his family provided an interview. Joanne phoned John's wife and explained that she wanted to speak with her about John and about the need for a Royal Commission into the scandal of child sexual abuse in the churches in the Hunter Valley region of New South Wales. She was cautious, however, about the potential risk to other victims of Denham. "It was a very carefully-worded article because I was terrified about other Denham victims also attempting suicide," she told me. "We worded it extremely carefully – to talk about the last time that [John and his wife] spoke which was a very loving sort of experience a couple of days earlier."

Once she had approval to publish the suicide note, McCarthy decided that John's haunting words "Too much pain" would make a powerful theme for the story and for what she expected might become ongoing coverage over the following months. She wrote about why victims became so desperate that suicide appeared to offer them the only escape from a living hell in which the authorities appeared to ignore the cries of children who needed protection from serial offenders. The theme of pain and the need for public truth-telling became the major arguments that McCarthy advanced for the need for a Royal Commission that could expose the truth. She said:

> Too much pain, became an explanation, and a demand for action coming from a man who'd died. Too much pain for too many people: now there is a need for the community to act, for government to act. This has gone on for too long.

Images of the missing man were also a powerful element in the news coverage. The missing person story included five photos – four in colour and one, of John as a child of about 8 years old, in black and white. The childhood photo had enormous impact.

Oh my god it was devastating. That was on our homepage and lots and lots of people commented to me that they saw that photo, and just died. That appeared in the newspaper but it was the online presence of it that was quite significant. People got it: 'Oh my god, these are crimes against *children*. That's in black and white.'

The juxtaposition of colour and black and white photographs was shocking because it illustrated that this was a crime against a boy in the 1950s and he was still trying to seek justice 50 years later. Again, the long time frame of the story exploded the 24/7 digital news cycle and became a piece of reportage that endured with sufficient gravitas to forge socio-political change.

Consideration was also given to the possible negative effects of the story of John Pirona's disappearance being published on victims of abuse. Before submitting the first article, Joanne sought support for any readers who might also be victims of Denham and contacted those she knew, to warn them of the impending publication. She also asked local policewoman Sergeant Kristi Faber for permission to publish the police officer's name at the end of the article so other victims could easily report to the police officer who was managing the case.[5] The officer agreed to do so. The first article ran front page and was shared widely on social media. It was picked up by the *Newcastle Herald's* sister capital city newspaper the *Sydney Morning Herald* and quickly gathered more readership.

Within days, John's body was found and the news coverage increased.[6] Joanne McCarthy could not write all the stories herself. She was also concerned about the risk of making herself too large a target for potential detractors. She asked a colleague at the *Sydney Morning Herald* to help her.[7] Also the political fallout of the story was gathering momentum. Police confirmed that three serving Catholic clergy were about to be charged. Calls came for a Royal Commission. The story was widely shared, and the audience grew very large, creating an example of Castell's "power of flows" – a groundswell of public support – that can produce a political response (Castells 2009). Within a week it was obvious to Joanne that there had to be a Royal Commission and she wrote an opinion article stating that "there will be a royal commission because there must be."[8] By then, she says, she was confident it was going to happen. John Pirona's suicide was the public face of the need for a Royal Commission. "In the end [his death] carried the need for a Royal Commission in the Hunter [Valley]," McCarthy said.

In her years of methodically reporting on the scourge of child sexual abuse, Joanne McCarthy had carefully and thoroughly laid the fire for change but it was an *ABC News* interview that lit the spark. ABC Television's current affairs programme *Lateline* broadcast an interview with police officer Detective Peter Fox who alleged that "from my own experience the Church covers up, silences victims, hinders police investigations, alerts offenders, destroys evidence and moves priests to protect the good name of the Church."[9] The detective's allegations combined with many years of research and reporting by other journalists created an unstoppable force for change. The then Australian Prime Minster Julia Gillard announced on 12 November 2012 that a Royal Commission would be held into institutional responses to the sexual abuse of children that had led to scores of suicides, hundreds of survivors receiving compensation – usually in secret 'hush money' settlements – and untold numbers of young lives devastated (Bowden 2012). It is unlikely that the Royal Commission would have eventuated without the national coverage and the consequent placement of the issue on the national political agenda. The effectiveness of the coverage in achieving a fourth estate outcome was due to a combination of strong analogue reporting skills and the amplification of the reporting via social media platforms that vastly increased the readership and the social demand and political will for governmental action to be taken.

Beyond Australia, Joanne McCarthy's investigations showed that offenders used the international network of the Catholic Church to escape prosecution. Church leaders could move offending clergy interstate or overseas to avoid scrutiny, to avoid apprehension or prosecution by law enforcement. McCarthy found that prolific Catholic paedophile Denis McAlinden, for example, had been back and forth from Australia to other countries, avoiding detection for decades. She said,

> They sent him to Papua New Guinea and New Zealand. He travelled to the Philippines, Ireland and England over a period of four decades. He was sent to get him out of the country after they had had complaints – then they would bring him back. They would send him interstate and then there would be complaints and they would bring him back to Newcastle – and they would flick him to another country and bring him back.

Victims of John Pirona's offender, John Denham, continued to come forward to police even after the Royal Commission ended. In 2019 Denham was convicted again, this time of raping a boy aged 10.[10]

Award

Joanne McCarthy won Australia's highest journalism accolade, the Gold Walkley Award in 2013, for her investigation. Her colleagues Chad Watson, Ian Kirkwood and Jason Gordon were joint winners with her of a second Walkley Award for Best Community and Regional Affairs Reporting.

Case study 4: *In my skin*

Direct interpersonal connections remain at the core of the best investigative journalism despite the availability of social media and other forms of digital connection. An example of this is the work of another regional reporter, *Geelong Advertiser* reporter Mandy Squires, who created powerful news coverage that was sparked by her own observations as a trainee teacher. Mandy Squires completed a journalism degree and worked for the *Geelong Advertiser,* but left to raise her children. While she was studying for a teaching degree, she undertook practice teaching in schools and noticed that students aged in their mid-teens seemed disengaged from their education and from the wider community. They also felt invisible in the media. She told me:

> They were so disengaged but they were the most entertaining, colourful fantastic group of kids ever – but really disinterested in education. I had them for quite some time and it really sparked my interest in young people and giving them a voice in the mainstream media.

"They came to know that I had been a journalist. They were interested in all the stories I had to tell from having been a journalist." Mrs Squires told the students about news stories she had written, court stories and colourful stories. Although the students listened, they complained that they did not see themselves in newspapers. They told her, "We would be more interested in them but we don't have a voice in them."

Mrs Squires was forced to stop her tertiary study when she was diagnosed with cancer in 2010. After chemotherapy treatment she needed an income and returned to her reporting job at the *Geelong Advertiser,* this time as education roundsman. After her teaching experience, she wanted to try to give teenagers a voice in the local media – to enable them to speak about the issues that were important to young people.

I went to a local high school, Belmont High, which is a very innovative school. I asked them if they would work with me in having Year Nine students write in their own words what it was like to be 14 and 15 and to be in their skin, and to talk about sexuality and peer pressure. They talked about families, relationships, their skin, school – everything that mattered to them – in their own words.

The teachers cooperated with her idea and for a year she ran writing sessions with the students during their English classes.

Mrs Squires' cancer treatment coincided with the final phase of editing and preparing the student work for publication. The stories were published while she was in hospital and colleagues helped her to check proofs in the days before she had further surgery. The student work was allocated eight pages in the newspaper every day for five days. Space limitations in the physical paper meant not all the work was published in hard copy but it was all published online.[11] Although the coverage began as an analogue idea, it was digital technology that enabled it to be published despite the reporter being in hospital. The collaboration between the newspaper and the school was created informally by a reporter and teachers, and then endorsed by the newspaper management and the school administration. Brokering collaborations between media outlets and organisations is in its infancy and there are no recognised template contracts for collaboration. Achieving a workable collaboration therefore depends upon the initiative and interpersonal skills of the reporter and organisation's representatives to attract the support of their respective managers. The *In my skin* project yielded positive change for the students who took part and for the community as a whole, in raising awareness of youth and community issues.

One of the student stories was especially poignant. A Sri Lankan asylum-seeker student wrote movingly about feelings of distress at being ostracised by other students. She wrote that she had never been invited to anything. She wanted to be included. She thought she should be more used to being left out, but it still hurt. The *Geelong Advertiser* published one quote from her story on the front page of the newspaper, in white text on a black background. "It was heartbreaking. I cannot even barely tell you now without welling up," Mrs Squires said.

Reader engagement with the student articles was high, and reaction was very positive towards the project and also towards the young people who took part. "We had leading Australian psychologists, Headspace, and lots of different agencies that were really supportive of the project. I don't think we had any negative responses. They were very overwhelmingly positive." In addition, the coverage gave an outlet to teenagers whose voices had been largely silent in the public arena.

> It showed young people in a light of being so articulate and having this really important voice that was never really in the mainstream media – we just did not listen to it – and when we did for a week, it was really interesting what we learned.

One student who showed special interest and significant ability was invited to become a columnist for the newspaper after the project concluded. She wrote every week about teen issues and provided a youth perspective on local issues.

Award

In my skin was selected as a finalist in the Walkley Awards for Coverage of Community and Regional Affairs and was adopted as part of the English section of the Australian National Curriculum. The impact of the *In my skin* writing project was so great that it was continued in subsequent years and was adopted as a trial curriculum component for the national curriculum. The trial was so successful that it became part of the Australian National Curriculum for Year Nine.[12]

Analogue skills in the digital age

The investigative reporting by Nicky Phillips, Michael Bachelard, Joanne McCarthy and Mandy Squires all required analogue skills: face-to-face interviews, shoe leather journalism, making and maintaining news contacts and building a network of contacts. None of these analogue skills is displaced by digitisation but each can be enhanced and adapted for the digital age.

Face-to-face interviews

Building trust with new news sources is still best achieved face to face – preferably in person, but still achievable online. Richard Baker believes nothing can replace *being* somewhere or *being with* someone in person:

> For us to win someone's trust, it is far easier to do that by making the effort to go and see them. You might need to do that three or four times before they agree to tell their story or give you the information that they are sitting on. It is human nature – if

someone has got something that is highly damaging to someone else, particularly if they are in power and this person is taking a great risk to blow the whistle, we owe them time and owe them the basic good manners to build trust.

Face-to-face interviewing will remain best practice but the availability of technologies that facilitate face-to-face interviewing are being relied upon more heavily by investigative journalists – especially since the onset of the COVID-19 pandemic in early 2020 – when they need to interview people face to face but can't be physically face to face due to health risks, or constraints of time or money or distance.

Given the risk of metadata exposing a whistleblower, face-to-face interviews are one of the safest ways to ensure anonymity and avoid leaving digital footprints. However, according to Nicky Phillips, sources can also be protected by using temporary email accounts. To do this, the reporter sets up an email account for which the reporter and news sources have the address and password to log in. Both can draft emails which the other person can read and respond to as a draft without any email actually being sent. "In this way, emails can be written and read by both parties but there is no metadata able to be detected because no email is sent," she says. Once the article is published the email account can be shut down.

Shoe leather journalism

Shoe leather journalism played a significant role in all the investigations in this book. The *Concrete Creek* investigation, examined in more detail in Chapter 5, was physically intensive, with the reporters bushwalking in rugged and mountainous terrain to verify the extent of damage from a mining operation in a national park. The trekking was arduous, but the mapping of global positioning system (GPS) points and the video evidence obtained persuaded the government to order the mining company to repair extensive environmental damage in a conservation area.

Making and maintaining news contacts

The story leads that resulted in the investigations in this book were discovered by reporters from both known and unknown contacts, or a public event, or from personal experience. Only four of the 14 stories were sparked by news sources already known to the reporter. Interestingly, six of the investigations were initiated by news sources *selecting* and contacting a reporter. In each case the reporter built trust and a strong rapport with the previously unknown source. Two of the stories were triggered by public events and one was sparked by personal experience. The news-source initiated stories in this book include landmark investigations such as Joanne McCarthy's *Shine the light* series and the Waddington investigation. Another two of the investigations were also precipitated by unknown whistleblowers. The ability of whistleblowers to contact a selected reporter, in any country, highlights the importance of reporters being contactable online.

Despite the growing emphasis on online data sources, participants in this book continue to rely heavily, although not exclusively, on physical documents for verification of information and data. Audio recording devices and data storage are also becoming so miniaturised and inexpensive that they are easily accessible. Covert audio and video recording are also relatively easy and inexpensive, an example is the *Secret tapes* investigation, discussed in Chapter 6, which relied on a whistleblower passing covertly recorded tapes to a reporter.

Network building

Analogue networks can be scaled up very quickly by digital networks, giving reporters national and international contacts with leaders in any field of endeavour via public social networks such as Twitter and private social networks that they build for a particular group of news sources.

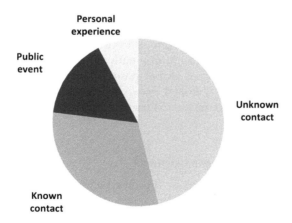

Figure 3.1 Unknown and known contacts as important sources of story leads
Source: Gearing 2016.

The skills to create and maintain personal and electronic networks are vital for investigative reporters in the digital age as these networks can far exceed the scope of analogue networks. However, analogue net-working-building skills can be adapted for building networks online, enabling reporters to expand their geographic reach to news contacts globally.

Despite the nascent cyber connections that are now possible, some of the most important and ground-breaking news investigations rely almost exclusively on personal contacts and face-to-face personal interaction both for the story lead and the verification and follow-up stories. Computerised communication alone cannot replace or improve the quality of connection found through personal connec-tions, human relationships, face-to-face contact or the veracity of official print records and digitised historical documents, public and private records and shoe leather journalism – the direct observation of events, people and places. Verification procedures in which physical records are obtained remain important in journalistic work despite the availability of new communications technologies. However, strong traditional investigative journalistic skills can be vastly enhanced by the use of new technologies for building networks between reporters and sources, reporters and other reporters and reporters and audiences.

Notes

1 Michael McKenna and Amanda Gearing. 2013. "Church's wall of silence on sexual abuse." *The Australian*. 10 May 2013.
2 Nicky Phillips. 2009. "Scientists discover three new Aussie dinosaurs." *ABC Science*. 3 July 2009. https://www.abc.net.au/science/articles/2009/07/03/2615729.htm.
3 Nicky Phillips. 2013. "Fossil hunters uncover a vast treasure trove at iso-lated site." Fairfax: *Sydney Morning Herald,* 3 August 2013. https://www.smh.com.au.
4 Joanne McCarthy. 2019. "Psychiatrist tells judge Denham, 77, 'never to have access to children' if he survives jail sentence when he's close to 90." Newcastle NSW, Newcastle Newspapers: *Newcastle Herald*. 28 February 2019. https://www.newcastleherald.com.au.
5 Joanne McCarthy. 2012. "Victim of paedophile priest missing, wife fears worst." Newcastle NSW, Newcastle Newspapers: *Newcastle Herald*. 25 July 2012. https://www.newcastleherald.com.au.
6 Joanne McCarthy. 2012. "Abuse victim's last sad words." Newcastle NSW, Newcastle Newspapers: *Newcastle Herald.* 27 July 2012. https://www.newcastleherald.com.au.
7 Linton Besser and Joanne McCarthy. 2012. "Calls multiply for inquiry into handling of sex abuse." Fairfax: *Sydney Morning Herald*. 1 August 2012.

8   Joanne McCarthy. 2012. "There will be a Royal Commission because there must be." Newcastle NSW, Newcastle Newspapers: *Newcastle Herald.* 3 August 2012. https://www.newcastleherald.com.au.

9   Tony Jones. 2012. Studio interview with Senior NSW Detective Peter Fox. *Lateline.* ABC Television.

10 Joanne McCarthy. 2019. "Psychiatrist tells judge Denham, 77, 'never to have access to children' if he survives jail sentence when he's close to 90." Newcastle NSW, Newcastle Newspapers: *Newcastle Herald.* 28 February 2019. https://www.newcastleherald.com.au.

11 "In my skin." 2012. *Geelong Advertiser.* 1 October 2012. http://sit.geelongadvertiser.com.au/in-my-skin.

12 Australian Curriculum. https://www.australiancurriculum.edu.au.

4 Investigative uses for social media platforms

> The beauty, and the fatal flaw of social media is that everyone can publish whatever they like.[1]

Journalism scholars have emphasised the distribution and potentially viral sharing of news stories. While wider distribution is a factor of social media platforms, the more important function is their use in investigation, connection and verification. Bim Atkinson's public blog post to a social media site in New Zealand, naming Waddington as a sadistic paedophile and also naming another teacher, Peter Gilbert, as a "Waddington-induced pedophile" enabled connections to be made that would have otherwise been all but impossible.[2] This needle-in-a-haystack find in a social media post yielded the name of a particular person – a victim of a crime by a particular offender. In the years before social media this search would probably not have even been attempted. A searchable social media post made the task almost instantaneous. Social media connections enabled victims who the Church appeared to believe would never be able to find each other, to make contact and to share their information. The success of making a connection meant that, in this case, an injustice that had waited 50 years to be aired could at last be reported and addressed. Something new is happening that is both important for individuals and for journalists, to be able to serve justice via news coverage in the public sphere. In this case the connection led to media coverage, accountability of individuals and organisational change in one of Britain's foundational institutions, bringing a measure of justice for victims of crime who had been denied it for decades.

Journalistic investigation is not restricted to the period before the story breaks – it may well continue afterwards. It seemed there must be many more victims, so I searched for key words that might lead to the mystery victim pictured in Waddington's study that Eli Ward had

DOI: 10.4324/9781003139980-4

hoped to find by being named and identified himself in a childhood photo and an adult photo. I was hoping to find another public social media post that might lead to any other victims. Just after midday on 12 May (Australian time) a search result located an anonymous post made to an English blog site from a self-declared victim. The anonymous victim posted that the claim by the former Archbishop David Hope that Waddington was "a broken, dying man"' was not true. As a victim of Waddington, the anonymous contributor wrote that he was a child who was being abused when the offender was supposedly dying. He knew Waddington's cancer had been in remission for some years and the offender had been on holidays to France, redecorating his house, driving his convertible to London to see a ballet at Covent Garden. He concluded that, "Knowing this, I find it very hard to believe that the Archbishop did not knowingly mis-lead the Australians." The victim identified himself only as a Former Stat (a member of the cathedral's statutory choir). I emailed the blog master, who forwarded my request to make contact with the author of the anonymous blog post. The victim was willing to be interviewed by the *Times* reporter Sean O'Neill in London. Sean was able to write a follow-up story directly disputing the Archbishop's claim made to Bim Atkinson to dissuade him from taking action against the offender.[3] This is a dramatic example of a Church leader diverting a victim from taking legal action by giving deliberately inaccurate information that they believe the victim cannot dispute. The willingness of the anonymous victim to contribute to the investigation clearly showed the depth of deception by Church officials of the victim, and the brazenness of a senior Church official to be dishonest in private and in public media comments.

The following two case studies show the importance of being able to quickly verify the identities of specific people and to prove their associations with others. In the first case study, there was strong competition between the reporters – who all discovered the same basic information at the same time – to find and verify a new angle on the story. In the *Firestorm* investigation, there was less time pressure but the challenge was tracking down specific people in a different country who were survivors of a natural disaster – in this case a bushfire.

Case study 5: Sport doping scandal

A government minister told reporters at a media conference that organised crime figures had allegedly infiltrated Australian football codes, supplying performance-enhancing drugs to players and fixing matches.[4] The shock revelations sparked a flurry of investigation. A young reporter for ABC Television's *7.30 Report*, Caro Meldrum-Hanna, who was assigned to the story did not know the people involved in the medical care of the football players or the administrators of the clubs. There was strong competition between print, radio, television and online reporters to find out which teams were involved. Who were the doctors? Who were the biochemists? Who were the players who had been allegedly taking the drugs? The journalists were under great pressure on a national story competing for a scoop from the same base knowledge given to them at the same time by the minister. "The chase was on for newspaper, radio and television reporters to 'dig fast' and 'dig deep' to find out which teams, players, doctors and biochemists were involved in taking performance-enhancing drugs," she told me. An additional challenge for the reporter was to hold the information exclusively until the story could be broadcast. Television current affairs has a much longer production timeframe than newspaper or radio because of the need to arrange interviews, travel to different locations for in-person interviews on camera, scripting of the programme, legal clearance and editing. This placed extra time pressure on the television reporters to work as quickly as possible to verify identities and facts so they could find new sources who might be willing to be interviewed.

Caro Meldrum-Hanna began her investigation by searching company records including online Australian Securities and Investment Commission (ASIC) data bases to identify club officials. Once she verified the main identities, she searched social media platforms for the key actors. She said,

> I was trawling Facebook. I was trawling YouTube and I was trawling Twitter and an old Myspace account, desperately trying to find photos of these people because I didn't know who they were, and I didn't know what their history was. So social media was absolutely vital. Once I could say who they were and show them, I got the interview with Steve Dank and the rest snow-balled from there.

Her ability to quickly prove the links between people for an initial story persuaded a key news source to agree to an important follow up interview. She told me:

> I did not think I was going to get the interview with him, but he saw [the first programme]. I am pretty sure he watched it, or at

least his barrister did, and I had a conversation with him the day after that story was broadcast. Obviously it showed that I had done my research and I was the only one to have put these links together.

Her ability with this and other stories led to her moving to ABC Television's flagship investigative reporting programme *Four Corners* where she has undertaken complex investigations and won several more national awards for her work.

Another reporter, Richard Baker, from rival news outlet Fairfax, attended the same media conference that had aired the ministerial allegations about a football club breaking anti-doping rules. After the conference Richard had a call from a contact who tipped him off to a possible supplier of drugs to the club, who was allegedly a convicted drug trafficker. The story broke the next day, on 7 February 2013, revealing that convicted drug trafficker Shane Charter had allegedly supplied illegal substances to the Essendon Football Club via their sports scientist Stephen Dank.[5] That story brought more whistleblowers forward, and Richard Baker and his colleague Nick McKenzie followed up the new information to try to work out why the club had come to the attention of the authorities and whether the alleged drugs were banned substances. Their stories exposed corrupt customs officers at Sydney Airport that led to an internal investigation of the Customs and Border Protection Service, and revealed compromising links between the Victorian police and high-ranking members of bikie gangs.[6]

Awards

Caro Meldrum-Hanna won a Walkley Award in 2013 for All Media Sports Journalism for her series of reports exposing the use of drugs in sport. She has embraced new technologies and has won several awards either alone or in collaboration with colleagues for news coverage that created socio-political change. In a 2015 investigation she used facial recognition technology and GPS locations to analyse covert vision that revealed that greyhounds were being 'live baited.' Caro Meldrum-Hanna's investigation into the treatment of children in a detention centre sparked a Royal Commission.

Richard Baker and Nick McKenzie won two Walkley Awards in 2013, one for Best Coverage of a Major News Event or Issue for their collaborative coverage of the Essendon drug scandal, and the other for Best Print/Text News Report for three collaborative investigative reports on drugs and guns being smuggled through airports. The two reporters work as a very successful collaborative team and have won many Walkley Awards and made a significant contribution to exposing corruption in various government and business enterprises and defending freedom of the press.

Case study 6: *Firestorm*

Grandparents Tim and Tammy Holmes fled with their grandchildren into the ocean as a raging bushfire consumed the township of Dunalley in Tasmania on 4 January 2013. From their hiding spot under a jetty, Tim Holmes took photos of his wife holding the youngest of the five children in the water with them sheltering under a jetty from ember attack. The smoke is chokingly thick and the atmosphere has an eerie red hue cast by the nearby fire front that was consuming the rural district. Tim Holmes posted the photos to social media to let their family know they and the children were safe. The photos were quickly shared by mainstream media and social media. It was a British newspaper that followed up the story. Here we see a personal post of some photos becoming the story lead for a major international reporting project. The *Guardian* chose the project because they were preparing to open an office in Australia and they were looking for compelling Australian stories to tell to Australian readers. They also wanted a story that would resonate with readers in the UK. Producer Madhvi Pankhania outlined the aim of the project:

> We wanted to do a long-term project and we really wanted to work quite closely with them, take videos of the family, interview them and get the sense of how they were feeling on the day. It was an interactive project when we take a lot more time to really delve into a topic.

Staff at the *Guardian* in London made contact with the Holmes family and asked if they would be willing to co-operate with a team of reporters and multimedia technicians to create a multimedia presentation on the fire and its aftermath.

The family agreed and *Guardian Australia* commissioning editor Katharine Viner initiated the project and assigned a team of 22 reporters and technical staff to work on it. Reporter Jon Henley interviewed the grandparents, parents and children and also firefighters and other Dunalley residents. He wrote the script for a multimedia presentation called *Firestorm,* which included text, photographs, video, audio and graphics, that was published four months after the fire in May 2013.

Central production team member Madhvi Pankhania came to Australia in preparation for the launch of the Australian website and used her knowledge and connections with the website team in London to ensure the Australian website had all the technical support needed to launch the multimedia project as the *Guardian* launched in Australia. The production combines a detailed and compelling human interest story about the family's experience during the firestorm with information and advice about preparation for survival in natural disasters and the work of emergency services during crises (Henley et al. 2013). The interactive multimedia story is an early example of pro-active global investigative journalism informing readers in Australia and overseas about the increasing climate risk caused by climate change and how climate change is having severe short and long-term effects on people who are exposed to climatic extremes and natural disasters. ABC Television's *7.30 Report* also produced a follow-up story on the family six months after the fire (Bennett 2013).

Award

Writer Jon Henley and videographer Laurence Topham worked with a team of researchers, editors, designers, interactive developers, multimedia producers and sound engineers to produce *Guardian Australia's Firestorm* that won the Walkley Award for Best Multimedia Storytelling.[7]

Social media communications may be synchronous (that is, happening at the same time) or they may be asynchronous (that is, happening at different times). The asynchronous potential of social media connections means that the parties to a conversation don't have to be available – or even awake – for the message to be sent and received satisfactorily in any time zone. As these brief case studies show, social media enable investigations that were impossible, or at least likely to be very time-consuming via analogue methods. The reporters featured in this book have collectively used social media for 13 different investigative practices and routines.

Emerging investigative techniques

1. Finding names and verifying identities

A key task of investigations is to confirm the identity of individuals and their connections with other people and organisations, businesses or places. Combinations of internet data with social media platform searches can reveal associations between individuals which, in some cases, those individuals may be trying to hide. Stories can emerge when there is evidence that a person's claims of identity or their social connections are not true. This process is often exhaustive and very time-consuming using analogue methods.

2. *Communicating with isolated news sources*

Stories are more frequently emerging at the instigation of news sources who choose to make contact or give data or documents to a reporter in a home or foreign country, based on the reporter's published work. For example, scientists in isolated work environments have become a source of daily news leads for *Geelong Advertiser* reporter Mandy Squires who relies on Twitter to communicate with isolated scientists and finds two or three good story leads a week.

One of the earliest examples of the use of social media for finding unnamed but specific contacts was described by foreign correspondent Michael Bachelard who used online forums and chatrooms to find news contacts in his reporting on a religious sect known as the Exclusive Brethren in 2004. Mr Bachelard did not expect his story to prompt dozens of other victims to contact him via an early online chatroom. However, so many victims of the sect came forward over the next two years that Bachelard decided to compile a book (Bachelard 2008).

Twitter was an important source of information for journalists reporting during the 2008 Mumbai terrorist attacks in Bombay, India, both *to gather* information and *to report*, as James Campbell explained,

> Twitter works both ways for journalists. It can be for us to find out things that are going on, particularly on the spot – and it's also a way for us to show what we are doing … A lot of it was live coverage and people were drawing on what people were tweeting in the street.

People inside restaurants and hotels subjected to the attack were able to tweet from their rooms or hiding places as one of the hostages did:

> im locked inside Vitthals restaurant with a few frnds. shutters down. this is as close as i can get to the action #mumbai
> (Oh, Agrawal and Rao 2013, 425)

Members of the public who were caught up in the attack suddenly became legitimate, active witnesses who were using Twitter to report on the Mumbai terror attacks. This was one of the earliest examples of Twitter being used for newsgathering. Twitter now regularly carries official government messages, crisis information and political messages.

3. Finding unnamed but specific individuals

Social media platforms can help journalists to make contact with specific types of people much more quickly than was previously possible. Statistics and medical stories, for example, are often illustrated by the use of case study stories. Previously these would be found via personal contacts, contacts of other reporters or through doctors. Social media now provides very quick and direct access to people and groups with particular illnesses or conditions who are likely to be willing to speak about their experience because they have already shared details on social media.

4. Piggybacking on larger networks to crowd-source

Reporters can leverage their connections by tapping into the larger established networks, such as the Twitter hashtags of people who have a large number of followers. Michael Bachelard described a technique for doing this. When he was in Australia reporting on the 2010 Federal election, he needed to find scrutineers to help him with a story about the reasons for a high proportion of informal votes. He recognised ABC political reporter Annabel Crabb as one of the most significant online 'hubs' in the field. After monitoring one of her Twitter hashtags, #scruti, he invited scrutineers to contact him about the messages that voters had written on informal votes at the booths where they were scrutineering and generated a story from the comments on informal ballots.

5. Speeding up investigations

The speeding up of investigations may not always be necessary but, when it is, social media can vastly speed up the time taken to locate specific people or their links with specific organisations or businesses, as illustrated by several of the case studies.

6. Verifying associations

While social media platforms have not made all stories possible, Fairfax investigative journalist Richard Baker believes social media networks can give reporters a starting point to verify allegations by revealing relationships that the individuals may be trying to conceal, such as criminal associations.

> Social media has not turned the impossible into the possible. But it has made a lot of stories – particularly stories where a journalist is trying to find out about relationships that perhaps people are trying to keep concealed, in terms of criminal associations; or people being in a certain place at a certain time; and also stories of an international nature.

The connections between people, if proven, can be enough to implicate individuals in anti-social, political, illicit sexual or criminal activity. These connections were difficult to establish with pictorial evidence before the era of social media and required witness evidence and sometimes private detection and photographic evidence. ABC Television *7.30 Report* journalist Caro Meldrum-Hanna's investigation of the football drug scandal required evidence of times, dates and associations. "[Social media] gives you faces to names and dates and where people were at particular times that you can verify," she said. The ability of private individuals to publish online on social media platforms and to take photographs and post them online makes it far more possible for reporters to track associations, to establish identities and, sometimes, to establish meetings of people at critical times on particular dates.

7. Building secret networks to gather and hold information

A further use of Facebook and other platforms is secret groups. Facebook allows users to create groups with a privacy setting of 'closed' or 'secret.' The secret setting conceals the names of the members of the group and conceals their posts, except to members of the group. The only publicly visible evidence of the secret Facebook group is the name of the group. A secret group can be used to gather information from a defined group of people whilst protecting them as sources and protecting the information from disclosure to the public or competing media outlets or journalists. Secret groups can be very useful for snowballing from a few contacts to many in order to gather information from groups or communities. For example, after a flash flood disaster I knew only two victims who were in the water at one of the locations but I created a secret group and added them, asking them to invite others they knew into the group who they knew had been affected. Half an hour after establishing the group, the two members had invited another eight people, and by the afternoon the group had 34 members. The membership grew to more than 40 by the next day. This enabled me to gather specific information or to gauge community sentiment or opinions quickly and easily. When I obtained aerial vision I was able to quickly obtain names and contact details for people in the vision by posting screen shots of people stranded on house roofs from the vision to the secret group. Within minutes of posting the photos, members of the group were able to identify and give the names of some of the people in the photos and voluntarily supplied their phone numbers. The same technique could prove very useful in other natural or manmade disaster situations or in conflict zones.

8. Being accessible globally to news sources

Crowd sourcing can be performed to find domestic or even international contacts using other platforms such as Twitter, especially when there is a significant breaking news story. The crash of MH370 on 8 March 2014 became worldwide news and reporters in many countries were trying to break new stories on the reason or circumstances surrounding the Boeing 777's disappearance with the loss of all crew and passengers. Readers contacted Caro Meldrum-Hanna after her initial report on the crash for *Four Corners*. [8] Viewers from other countries gave her more information that enabled her to break a subsequent story on the crash.[9]

Sources may follow several reporters on public social media platforms such as Twitter, LinkedIn or a Facebook page and then get in touch directly and arrange a private method of communication. Mandy Squires describes the tentative nature in which whistleblowers often approach reporters.

> You see that someone has followed you [on Twitter]. And then suddenly, a little bit later, they tweet to you about an idea. Sometimes they give you direct messages. A few stories have come from LinkedIn. People connect with me on LinkedIn and then send me a message.

These connections can be made at any time of day from most geographic locations. The reporter can respond to a question or comment at a convenient time from anywhere.

9. Monitoring overseas events and rival coverage

Several of the journalists in my research study described how they use social media platforms such as Twitter for monitoring active overseas events from Australia. Actively monitoring an event means that if a news story breaks, they are ready to follow it quickly. *Four Corners* producer Vivien Altman described how she uses selected hashtags and follows selected people in particular overseas geographic zones (in this case in Gaza during the 2014 Israel-Gaza conflict), even though she was not working on a story about the conflict at the time. Monitoring selected people and hashtags gives a sense of what is going on and advance notice of breaking stories in overseas newspapers. Although the research was not for a particular story, Mrs Altman said the close monitoring of an overseas event via social media provided background knowledge of the conflict that is useful in future stories.

10. *Copy-testing live online*

Live online copy-testing is antithetical to the accepted news paradigms of breaking news first, or finding exclusive stories. However, now that news can be tweeted by any member of the public to an audience, the tweeting of news by reporters at events such as court cases or inquiries is now accepted as a regular practice. The benefit of tweeting during proceedings is not just an increased Twitter following but a refinement of story angles which has been shown anecdotally to increase the readership of stories. Fairfax reporter Sarah Whyte describes how her experience of live-tweeting news events changed how she views scoops and competition and her Twitter network. Ms Whyte experimented with live tweeting from an inquiry and found that her effort was rewarded by providing notes of proceedings, immediate audience feed-back and more Twitter followers. Tweeting during a hearing was not distracting once she became used to it and her tweets formed a set of notes she used to remind herself of the content and prompted her to think about interesting story angles. She also monitored the number of retweets of her original tweets, to see which pieces of evidence had attracted the most reader interest. Over time she discovered two useful strategies: first, there was a high correlation between a tweet that attracted a lot of retweets and a story based on that tweet attracting a large online readership. Secondly, she found that if a tweet started attracting a lot of retweets, it was worth writing the story immediately for the online newspaper rather than waiting for the print edition.

11. *Using social media platforms as a communications carrier*

Despite his continuing reticence to use social media platforms in his reporting, Fairfax correspondent Ben Doherty did use YouTube in an unconventional way to file video packages back to Australia when he was in locations with poor internet connection. During his time in Afghanistan in 2013 and 2014 internet connections frequently dropped out. He resorted to using YouTube to upload his files as private files which could be downloaded by staff in Australia, thereby overcoming the need for expensive satellite phone connections. Anyone who has worked remotely from their office will identify with the frustration of having worked on a story and completed it, only to have trouble filing it to a deadline from a remote location. Doherty was shown how to upload his work to YouTube on a private setting which his office could then access and download using ripping software. Based on this success, this method was used repeatedly in similar situations. YouTube became a private sharing platform that enabled Doherty to file from a war zone when internet connectivity was poor or patchy.

12. Deciding whether to hold a scoop for the print edition

The ease with which people can publish on social media sites means stories are at risk of leaking before being published. This means newspaper editors are less likely to hold a story for the front page unless they are sure it is exclusive. *Newcastle Herald* reporter Matt Carr monitors the Facebook accounts of people connected with any exclusive story that is being held for the print edition. If the story appears in social media, the paper will publish online instead of holding for their print edition. Even if a story breaks on social media, the effect can be to boost newspaper sales because interest in the story builds from social media platforms, driving higher sales of the physical newspaper.

13. Maintaining contact with official news sources

Journalists have traditionally relied primarily on official authorities as reliable news sources. This reliance has transferred to official digital sources. In a study of news sources used by major US news outlets in 2010–2011, Moon and Hadley (2014, 299) found that mainstream media "relied more on the Twitter feeds of traditional official sources than on those of non-official sources." They also found that TV cited Twitter accounts of traditional official sources 176 times (75.5 per cent) while newspapers cited them 52 times (62.7per cent) (Moon and Hadley 2014, 300). The adoption of Twitter by many politicians and government authorities has meant political journalists need to monitor Twitter streams for public announcements.

Despite the enormous opportunities for online networking, face-to-face interactions remain important for exclusive news stories. Indonesian correspondent Michael Bachelard willingly uses social media platforms, but he still finds that his personal contact with asylum seekers enables him to compete effectively to report asylum-seeker issues.

> I've got contacts because I went out to where their boats sank, and they were brought dripping back to shore by immigration depart-ment officials and put into a scummy hotel three hours' drive from Jakarta. I met them and interviewed them and talked to them – that's shoe leather. I'm not trying to privilege shoe leather over anything else, but I've subsequently become Facebook friends with a lot of those people, and they keep me in contact on Facebook.

His personal contacts, once established, are easy to maintain online, in effect value-adding his previous investment of time and effort in shoe leather reporting by giving him follow-up stories.

Globalising news

The use of social media platforms for all the above tasks indicates that social media platforms are becoming far more important sources of con-tacts and news leads as well as sources of evidence verification, no matter whether the stories are being written for a local, national or international publication. The divisions of local, state, national and international news are becoming blurred, especially in developed countries where the popu-lation is predominantly well connected via the internet. Citizens can follow breaking news overseas as closely as reporters, using suitable Twitter hashtags and using plain English searches for YouTube videos of breaking news events. According to Ben Doherty, major news stories can reach a global audience via a combination of mainstream media and social media platforms, irrespective of where the event is happening,

> A good story is a good story on whichever side of the world it is. I think all of the elements that apply to foreign news also applied to domestic news. In a first world country like Australia, perhaps even more so because you have such a connected community. People are on the Internet 24 hours a day and so they are much more accessible and much more plugged into those things.

Despite returning to Australia after working as a foreign correspondent, Ben Doherty is continuing to write stories that have an international aspect to them, reflecting the shift towards an increasingly globalised interconnected world.

Stories with wide potential reader interest are increasingly being conceptualised and written with a possible global audience in mind. In some cases, slow-moving issues such as pollution or climate change are humanised by engaging reader interest in a lead character in the story. For example, a story about the increasing amount of rubbish floating in oceans contrasted two sailing trips from Australia to Japan several years apart. Matt Carr told me how senior reporter Greg Ray's story 'The Ocean is broken' (Ray 2013) brought a slow-moving issue into the public sphere and attracted thousands of readers. The story is about a Newcastle sailor who sailed from Melbourne to Japan and back 10 years after a previous trip and invites the reading audience to see the world through the eyes of the sailor; to feel his sadness at the loss of sea life and the accumulation of non-biodegradable plastics in the ocean.

It is difficult now to imagine journalism without the influence of social media technologies. The application of networking power in investigative journalism holds enormous and exciting potential to rebalance the power of individuals with organisations, businesses and governments.

Adoption and advantages of social media techniques

Despite the power of social media platforms in investigations, the level of engagement with social media amongst my study cohort ranged from deliberate non-engagement to active daily engagement. Mandy Squires, for example, believes the opportunities to access people quickly and efficiently is unprecedented in her 20 years as a journalist and are a very effective way to gather information. Fairfax Parliamentary press gallery reporter Sarah Whyte believes social media is a natural evolution in journalism which should be used. However, many experienced reporters may not realise the full potential of using social media platforms to conduct journalistic investigations. This research is therefore timely and important. Of the reporters who participated in it, most had only been on Twitter for six months or less but some, including Madhvi Pankhania, discovered it to be "one of the most vital pieces of technology that there is out there."

Reluctance to engage with social media platforms

Although social media platforms were invented in the early 21st century and have quickly attracted very large public user numbers, many reporters have been reluctant to engage. The overwhelming reluctance and ambivalence of some reporters and media companies to engage with social media platforms has, arguably, constrained the potential of investigative journalism to carry out its fourth estate role. Reporters who have engaged with the digital age have overcome institutional bias against social media platforms in addition to their own fears about the technology and their perception of the legal risks. It is notable that for many of the reporters in this book, engagement with various social media platforms only came about through a specific need during their work on a particular story to use a social media platform to pursue a story. Significantly, all the reporters said they were self-taught or had help from colleagues. Not one of the research participants said their workplace was the main instigator or provider of their training in how to use social media platforms as a journalistic tool. However, all the participants said they wanted to know more about how to use social media platforms in their work. Some requested that the findings of this research should be written as a book to disseminate the new knowledge as widely as possible in the industry. Having engaged successfully with a social media platform, however, the reporters immediately were able to see more potential and powerful uses of the technology for *finding* information and news contacts in addition to disseminating their news stories. Facebook, for example has 2.7 billion active users making it a vast database of personal information that is freely available.[10] The enormous number of people who are active users of these platforms makes them a readily accessible resource for reporters.

Training in investigative techniques using social media platforms

In recent years systematic training programmes in using social media platforms for investigative journalism have begun to be written and delivered, mostly online. For example, the Knight Center produces free online courses for journalists and members of the public. One of their new courses in 2020 teaches digital investigations for journalists including how to follow the digital trail of people and entities.[11] New online tools are also emerging that enable forensic investigation of social media platforms. For example Tineye.com is a free reverse image search tool; Picodash.com can be used to search Instagram; YouTube-DataViewer.com, produced by Amnesty International, is an online tool that allows users to submit a URL to a YouTube video and receive metadata about the video including the number of views, date and time of upload, licence information and still images from the video that can be used to perform a reverse image search to verify its origin.[12]

Going global

The distinction between domestic and global investigative journalism has become less clear as the global reach of social media platforms has become seamlessly incorporated into social media platforms. Domestic news may, for example, suddenly become global depending upon the news values inherent in the story: impact, timeliness, prominence, proximity, the bizarre, conflict, currency and human interest. Domestic events as common as traffic, train or plane accidents with casualties, frequently have international links that require the reporter to contact next-of-kin in another country, changing the story from simply domestic news into a story that may gather an international audience.

The asynchronous nature of social media platforms enables journalists to maintain 'always on' two-way communication with news contacts, audience members and their media outlet. Asynchronous communication can vastly speed up the progress of an investigation, especially across time zones.

Coverage of sensitive and controversial issues

Several of the reporters believe they have greater access to news sources that allows them to report on sensitive topics more easily due to the investigative capabilities of social media platforms. Fairfax investigative reporter Sarah Whyte believes her engagement with social media platforms has given her more potential and ability to tell stories about sensitive or controversial issues, especially on her immigration round amongst asylum seekers who move between countries and often have no fixed address during their migration. Sarah simply tweets news and then tweets a link to her story. She found that many asylum seekers engaged with Twitter following selected hashtags to monitor changes in policy and legislation in their target countries. Her consumer affairs round also attracted a large Twitter following in a short time, increasing her Twitter followers from 1,000 to 2,800 people in five months. One story she posted on the day I interviewed her, received 79 tweets in the first hour. ABC Television reporter Caro Meldrum-Hanna also believes social media platforms provide more potential for reporters to tell stories that are sensitive or controversial "because you can actually get to the names and the faces. You can find people who are not otherwise named," she said. Using a court document, a person's geographic location, their age and basic details such as the school they went to, it is possible to discover a social media profile and find that person through social media and then send them a private message.

Building audience-reporter engagement

Until the evolution of social media, journalists may have rarely received feedback to their stories. The long hours, the difficult nature of investigations, the risks endured can feel undervalued. The advent of social media means reporters can receive immediate and substantial reader response to their work that may be either positive or negative. Positive feedback can be highly motivating and provide a sense of job satisfaction. "You can easily show what you've done. I've had to miss a lot of dinners but I just say 'Well actually I was writing a front page story which you can see tomorrow.'" For Sarah, the downside of the job has a complementary upside.

> My article is one of the top articles online – which I've just written. People are tweeting me. You get instant communication and instant feedback from people. So when you put in those long hours you get a lot out of it.

But she also warns that the long hours are unsustainable in the longer term and she needs to be careful not to burn herself out.

Risks of using social media platforms in investigative journalism

All the reporters interviewed perceived risks in using social media platforms for investigations either alone or in combination with other investigative methods. The disadvantages included the risk that the story might leak, destroying their exclusivity; the risk of inaccuracy of source material posted to a social media platform; the risk to personal safety; and legal risk. Mandy Squires suggests that selected details only should be shared to a restricted audience. "You have got to put it up in such a way that only people you want to see, can see it." She also says any post also needs to avoid tipping off other reporters to the investigation. "If they know that is how you are gathering information, they watch," she warns. Caro Meldrum-Hanna has found a similar balance between using social media to gather information against the risk of leaking her story ideas. "The problem is maintaining privacy of your investigation, of your source and the content of what you are discussing," she says. Social media posts should never be used as a primary source without thorough fact-checking, "People have been undone from following stuff on Twitter, so you have to be very wary." These risks can be successfully mitigated by being careful about sharing details of an active investigation to preserve exclusivity.

Reporting deaths

Long-established procedures between police and reporters, such as waiting for police to confirm deaths and injuries in accidents are being overturned or by-passed by the use of social media platforms. Reporters can sometimes contact grieving families before police officially release names and other identifying information. Reporters and/or the newspaper's lawyers must then decide whether to publish or to wait for police confirmation. The *Newcastle Herald* has managed this risk by having an informal agreement with police that if the reporters discover identifying information, they liaise with police to ensure next of kin have been identified before reporting a death. *Newcastle Herald* reporter Matt Carr said the immediacy of social media could cause friction between reporters and police because if reporters are looking in the right places, they can usually find a grieving local family quite quickly. "I guess that opens up a bit of an ethical door, but quite often we will talk to the police, and try and get confirmation but also give them the time that they need to notify the family."

A deadly profession

Journalists around the world experience danger, imprisonment, injury and occasionally accidental or deliberate deadly force in the course of their work. The Committee to Protect Journalists keeps records of reporters who are missing, or who have been imprisoned or killed: 1,388 journalists were killed in the course of their work between 1992 and 2020, either by being murdered, being caught in crossfire or conflict, or while they were on a dangerous assignment.[13] Other journalists are imprisoned or remain missing. The Committee to Protect Journalists reported that 248 journalists were imprisoned in 2019; and 64 journalists were reported missing in 2020. In countries with repressive regimes, reporters may be imprisoned, surveilled or be restricted from internet and social media access.[14] The Dart Center for Journalism and Trauma provides free safety training for working in hostile environments such as war zones, disaster zones and other dangerous locations and undertakes research and reports on current safety training and the need for safety training (Slaughter et al. 2017).

Legal risks

Reporters who post to social media generally do so without the backup checks by sub-editors or in-house lawyers. Anyone who posts to social media needs to be aware of the legal risks, such as defamation, when posting comments or information online. Criminal defamation offences can carry jail terms if the publisher is proven to know the material to be false or if the writer or publisher has published without regard as to whether the matter is true or false; and if a prosecutor is able to prove an intention to cause harm to a person.

Mitigating the risks

The risks of using social media platforms for journalistic investigations can be mitigated relatively easily by remaining dedicated to journalistic ethics and values including checking facts and ensuring sources are reliable. The risk of inaccuracy and the risk of a story leaking can both be overcome. If the facts of a story cannot be established, the risk of inaccuracy can be entirely mitigated by holding the story until the facts are established or disproved. *Newcastle Herald* reporter Donna Page gave an example of the paper's online editor acting this way. Despite the perceived urgency of reporting a major fire and that other news outlets had already published the story, a reporter who held the story was vindicated when it was discovered that the reported fire had, in fact, not occurred. As Donna said:

> [Our police reporter] was saying 'No. We are not running with that. We have not got that confirmed.' Despite the apparent urgency of getting to press, the reporter had no authoritative source, such as a fire commander or an eyewitness. And no photographs. And the thing had not burnt down. He held his line and he was right.

Fact checking and source checking remain vital. Ben Doherty says it pays to be sceptical of anything published on Twitter unless it comes from a reliable source. "If it is coming from someone I trust, I will rely on that. If you are hearing things from different sources that are not collaborating – that again is further evidence of its verisimilitude."

Techniques for using social media platforms for investigations enable reporters to build larger, more responsive global networks of news contacts. Assuming that reporters have analogue skills in developing rapport with news sources, interviewing, verifying information and writing, then those journalists with more networked social media connections are more likely to find stories and to be found by news sources who have important stories to tell. Reporters can connect quickly, easily and cheaply with people and groups to find information and connections that have previously been too difficult or slow to find or too costly. Building a global network of news contacts enables reporters to act at times as a global fourth estate, highlighting injustice for attention by various authorities. Risks of using social media platforms for investigative journalism do exist but these can be minimised, thus leading to an overall increase in the opportunities to tell compelling controversial and sometimes sensitive stories that can have a significant social impact. Those reporters who build purpose-designed digital networks of contacts and who use social media platforms can work faster and more effectively to find and verify stories than was previously possible.

Notes

1 Matt Carr. PhD research interview. 2014.
2 B. Atkinson. n.d. "Memories from St Barnabas Boarding School, Ravenshoe Nth Qld." [Blog post]. Retrieved from www.oldfriends.co.nz. The website was archived in 2016 by the National Library.
3 Sean O'Neill, Michael McKenna and Amanda Gearing. 2013. "Former Archbishop of York 'covered up' sex abuse scandal." London, News UK: *The Times*. 10 May 2013. www.thetimes.co.uk.
4 Simon Cullen and Ben Atherton. 2013. "Doping probe rocks Australian sport." *ABC News*. 26 April 2013. https://www.abc.net.au.
5 Richard Baker, Nick McKenzie and Cameron Houston. 2013. "Club link to drug dealer." Melbourne, *The Age*. 7 February 2013. https://www.theage.com.au/sport/afl/club-link-to-drug-dealer-20130206-2dz05.html.
6 Richard Baker and Nick McKenzie, selected news reports in 2012 and 2013: "Airport in grip of drug trade," 20 December 2012; "Smuggled guns: customs officers lied about scan," 21 December 2012; "When the good guys go bad," 21 December 2012; "Drug suspicions over Essendon grow," 4 July 2013; "Essendon fears drug deceit," 27 July 2013; "Dons told drug was not legal," 31 July 2013. Melbourne, *The Age*.
7 J. Henley, K. Viner, L. Glendining, M. Pankhania, F. Panettas, J. Richards and M. Khalil. 2013. "Firestorm." Australia, Guardian Media Group: *Guardian*. 23 May 2013.
8 Caro Meldrum-Hanna and Wayne Harley. 2014. "LOST: MH370." *Four Corners*, ABC Television. 19 May 2014.
9 Caro Meldrum-Hanna. 2014. "Malaysia Airlines flight MH370: family of Captain Zaharie Ahmad Shah defends his reputation." *Four Corners*, ABC Television. 20 May 2014.
10 "Monthly active users worldwide as at the third quarter of 2020." Statistica.com. https://www.statista.com/statistics.
11 Craig Silverman, Brandy Zadrozny, Jane Lytvynenko and Johanna Wild. 2020. "Digital investigations for journalists: how to follow the digital trail of people and entities." https://journalismcourses.org.
12 Andrea Carson. 2016. "How investigative journalists are using social media to uncover the truth." *The Conversation*. https://theconversation.com.
13 Committee to Protect Journalists. 2020. https://cpj.org/data/killed.
14 "10 most censored countries." 2020. Committee to Protect Journalists. https://cpj.org/reports/2019.

5 Investigative uses for Web based communications

Email, online archiving, online searching

Four published obituaries in two regional and two national newspapers in England honoured the late Dean of Manchester describing him as a dedicated priest who had worked in Australia in the 1950s and 1960s and then returned to England, rising to senior positions in the Church until his retirement as Dean of Manchester Cathedral in 1994.[1] In addition to verifying career details, the obituaries raised the possibility that Waddington could have been detected offending in the 1950s and sent to Australia as a result. The young priest with a blue-ribbon education from Cambridge University was initially posted to a London parish but after only a short time he was sent to Australia to a school in regional Queensland as chaplain – certainly not a promotion. Waddington's career path was typical of paedophile offenders in that each of his roles had provided him with trusted access to children – first as a school chaplain and then headteacher – despite his lack of any educational qualifications. Once back in England, Waddington was appointed General Secretary of the General Synod Board of Education in Britain and then Dean of Manchester. As Dean, he personally supervised the boys in the two Cathedral choirs. One of the obituaries even ventured that Waddington "had a special gift for teaching boys, which proved useful in his later cathedral appointments when he had responsibility for choristers." It also stated that he was a member for over three decades of the Oratory of the Good Shepherd, a celibate order of Anglican priests and became its Superior.[2] This publicly available evidence verified relevant facts, despite the offender having died.

In the following three case studies each investigation relied on Web based communications: the first on the use of GPS to verify the exact location and extent of environmental damage; the second on international communications between two reporters working together from

DOI: 10.4324/9781003139980-5

different countries; and the third, a purpose-built encrypted cyber forum that allowed hundreds of reporters around the globe to collaborate on an investigation into a vast database of financial information. GPS is used extensively by the investigative journalism website Bellingcat which uses the technology to geolocate events and verify facts, particularly in Russia, Syria and Ukraine.[3]

Case study 7: *Concrete Creek*

A local bushwalker phoned *Newcastle Herald* reporter Donna Page in mid-2013 and told her some concrete had leaked from a controversial mine site located in a National Park. The mine had been approved despite 97 per cent of the mine footprint being in Sugarloaf State Conservation Area west of Newcastle, in New South Wales. Donna Page needed to see the area, but she was unable to trek to the rugged location at the time. She asked two of her colleagues to have a look. Reporter Matt Carr and photographer Darren Pateman went to the mine site and found large cracks in a mountain in extremely steep, dense bushland. Using GPS they logged the location of the cracks as they walked along ridges to verify what they thought was the extent of the damage. During the afternoon they reached a cliff face that had sheared off. Donna Page clearly recalls answering Darren's phone call, "He said to me 'You are not going to f***ing believe it.' This is far worse than we had any idea."

Donna Page phoned the mining company to give them a right of reply to what the others had found. Mining company staff assured her that the "minor subsidence" was already being addressed. Page was still not convinced; as she told me,

> I thought, there seems to be quite a large section there – and it wasn't restricted to the public – they had tape up with 'MINE SUBSIDENCE DO NOT ENTER.' Anyone could have entered there. It was just suspicious. My contact is a nature lover and is extremely connected to this part of the bushland. He is very passionate. I thought, there's more to this than what they're saying.

When the newspaper ran an initial story on the subsidence, a mining contractor read the story and phoned Donna Page.[4] He told her that there was far worse damage at the mine site than she had reported and alleged that a creek had been accidentally concreted after grout ran down a crack in the mountain and out the bottom, solidifying in a creek bed.

Darren Pateman and Matt Carr volunteered to go back to the mine site but this time they planned to approach the area from a different direction. Darren recalled seeing flashes of white in the bush far below when he had stood at the top of the cliff that had collapsed. He said,

> I went back again with the GPS and GoPro and still cameras. I knew from the first visit where the major cracks were, so I went in at the bottom of the Range the second time and guessed where that grout would have flowed out and we came straight into the grouted creek pretty easily.

Workmen who had pumped grouting into a large crack in the ground for two days had not realised the concrete was flowing out further down the cliff face and flowing into the creek. By activating his GPS and walking down the creek on the concrete spill to where the grout had stopped running, they were able to measure the distance as being 400 metres. The company had argued the spill ran for less than 200 metres. The logged GPS points verified the true extent of the damage.

The revelations were published on page one and wrapped to a double-page spread in the newspaper.[5] The following day the paper was able to reveal that the government had known about the damage but had not ordered the mine to repair the subsidence or clean up the concrete spill. The area had been cordoned off only with some tape. The story gained more exposure by being published in the *Sydney Morning Herald,* another Fairfax publication. Once the story was published to a capital city audience, it quickly gained political traction and was picked up by journalists around Australia and overseas. Reporters in the US phoned Donna Page and interviewed her about the story. In Australia, news crews from ABC and Channel 7 trekked into the site, assisted by local bushwalking guides.

The coverage led to New South Wales state Premier Barry O'Farrell instigating an intergovernmental investigation into the subsidence. The government also apologised publicly for keeping the subsidence damage from longwall mining a secret from the public. Legal action against the mining company forced the company to clean up the concreted creek. The remote and rugged nature of the location meant the clean-up had to be conducted by sending helicopters with teams of workers with picks and shovels into the site and airlifting the concrete out – a task that took nearly 12 months. In addition, new policies were introduced to ensure future public disclosure by the NSW Government of any environmental damage caused by mining companies.[6] The outcomes achieved by public disclosure of the damage resulted in repair of the creek and legislative changes which will reduce the likelihood of a similar disaster in future going undetected. The success of the *Concrete Creek* investigation led to the *Newcastle Herald* buying a GoPro camera for use by the newsroom.

Award

The *Concrete Creek* investigation coverage was shortlisted in the 2013 Walkley Awards for Best Coverage of Community and Regional Affairs.

Case study 8: *Bangladesh factory collapse with global aftershocks*

Fairfax reporter Sarah Whyte was consumer affairs reporter at the time a clothing factory, Rana Plaza, in Bangladesh collapsed in April 2013, killing 1,127 people. Reporting the story from Australia only would have been very difficult. Likewise, reporting the story from Bangladesh alone would have been difficult. Fairfax assigned two reporters: one in Australia and one in Bangladesh. Sarah's news editor wanted to find an Australian angle on the story and asked her to try to trace back garments for sale in Australia to see if they were from sweat-shop factories like the one that had collapsed. Foreign correspondent Ben Doherty who was based in Delhi, India, was in Sydney at the time. Sarah began the investigation by shopping at department stores in Melbourne and buying clothes with "Made in Bangladesh" labels. Ben flew to Melbourne to collect them from Sarah, and then flew back to Bangladesh with the garments to try to verify their factories of origin. Meanwhile Sarah Whyte began contacting the head offices of the Australian retailers where she had bought the clothing and asked them how many factories they had in Bangladesh. Once in Bangladesh, Ben located some of the factories where the clothes had been made. When he reported his findings to Sarah, she was able to directly challenge the Australian companies as to whether they knew the clothes they were selling were made in a sweat-shop factory in Bangladesh.

Ben Doherty described the synergies the reporters achieved by using several types of technology to communicate with each other and with the public during the investigation. He said,

> We would talk mainly by email, often by Skype, and we would also find reaction to stories and we would get comment on stories via Twitter. We would promote the stories online. She would promote. I would promote. People would give us feedback and would find other people for follow up stories. The internet and social media and Web based communication was crucial to all of that.

This investigation is an example of how digital disruption has facilitated journalistic investigation, enabling reporters to verify connections quickly that would have been very costly and time-consuming to prove using analogue methods.

Several factory collapses and fires in the previous couple of years in Bangladesh meant the issue of shoddily built factories and cheap labour was politically charged in Bangladesh. As the issues of low wages and lack of enforcement of building standards gained momentum, the two reporters shared their findings. The time zone difference between Australia and Bangladesh meant that even though each of the reporters rested overnight, the investigation itself was able to continue almost 24 hours a day. Each reporter sent their work to the other at the end of each day, giving each other leads for the following day and propelling the investigation forward. Ben described the benefit of the teamwork, "We're five or six hours behind in Bangladesh. I'd have new impetus in the morning because Sarah had done something during the day and got some reaction." The story progressed quickly but the pace was ramped up once the reporters discovered a rival news organisation, ABC's *Four Corners,* was also working on a story about the Rana Plaza collapse. The Fairfax team had to bring their deadline forward by a week. Sarah Whyte described the added pressure of the final phase of the investigation leading up to their first major publication.

> We had to really step it up. Ben would find evidence that Kmart or Woolworths had links – we were working very hard. Sometimes we would get our times zones mixed up and he would be calling me at 12 o'clock at night or I would phone him at 5 o'clock in the morning. So it was a very dynamic working relationship.

Sarah Whyte was surprised that retailers in Australia became more and more willing to give her information as the coverage continued. Retailers were so concerned about public perceptions of their ties with sweat-shop labour that pressure increased for them to be more transparent. "We had three stories on that first day (in June) but by the time it got to December we had written between 30 and 50 articles together." Sarah found that the more she went back to the companies, the more they started telling her how many factories they had and what the ethical sourcing was like and how it worked.

The articles published by Fairfax in Australia were picked up by other countries, including in Bangladesh, where the coverage precipitated a strike by poorly paid garment workers. The workers took the opportunity of the global media spotlight to try to gain improved pay and conditions. "The Bangladeshis had a garment strike and tried to get more money because they knew the global attention was on them and they used that to their advantage," she said. This rare opportunity for previously voiceless, powerless garment workers to become the focus of global media coverage gave them a voice in the globalised public sphere. The coverage in Australia, Bangladesh and other countries resulted in much-needed reforms including higher wages and better workplace safety for the employees.

Collaboration between the reporters vastly increased the speed of the investigation and the impact of the coverage. Ben Doherty said that verifying the workers were being used in sweat-shop labour conditions to produce clothes that were being sold in Australia elevated the story in the Australian media from a foreign news story that would have run in the foreign pages to a national domestic story that ran front page in Australia. As he explained, "A story saying 'Bangladeshi factories are terrible' is a page 13 world story. A story saying, 'Australian clothes are made in a terrible Bangladeshi factory' is a page 1 story." In addition, the impact of the story in Australia forged changes in consumer behaviour, with customers avoiding clothing made by sweat-shop labourers. The political impact in Bangladesh was dramatic and led to better government regulation of building standards for factories and higher wages for factory workers.

Award

Sarah Whyte and Ben Doherty won the Walkley Award in 2013 for All Media Social Equity Journalism for their coverage in the *Sydney Morning Herald.* [7]

Case study 9: *Tax haven investigation*

Irish-born reporter Gerard Ryle worked in Australia for 20 years, winning four Walkley Awards for his investigative reporting. In 2011 a whistleblower sent him an unsolicited parcel containing a hard drive with a cache of 2.5 million leaked digital files relating to offshore bank accounts. The data were far more than he could investigate single-handedly. Coincidentally, Gerard was appointed to be the director of the International Consortium of Investigative Journalists based in Washington in 2011. He took his hard drive with him. An investigation into the cache of financial files was first proposed late in 2011, when ICIJ members met at an investigative journalism conference in Kiev and 10 reporters expressed an interest in the potential of the data cache to generate story leads.[8] As the reporters left to return home, they needed to ensure communications and sharing of data would be secure. The ICIJ's information technology staff set up an encrypted cyber forum so the reporters could search and download relevant documents, communicate safely with each other and help each other with the technical aspects of the work (Walker Guevara 2014). Further security was arranged to encrypt emails. The names of key sensitive targets of the investigation were also code-named.[9]

The team grew over the following years into a team of 80 ICIJ reporters from 26 countries working collaboratively on the database of 28,000 pages of secret financial documents relating to 120,000 offshore companies and trusts in 170 countries.[10] The journalists were able to share interview transcripts, photographs and confidential information even though some of the reporters worked for rival news organisations in their home countries.[11] More than 500 individual tax rulings were indexed by country, company and other categories. The secure server also enabled reporters to upload new documents and video and audio material they had gathered (Keena 2014). The success of the first investigation into tax havens led to further investigations and eventually to the Panama Papers in 2016 and the Paradise Papers revelations in 2017. The computer networking hardware and software developed in the first investigation were ready and available to work on in subsequent data caches. The long arc of these investigations, from 2011 until 2017 and the legal and political fallout of the investigations is notable, especially in an age of livestreamed news as it happens and the transitory nature of stories in the 24/7 news cycle.

Virtual newsroom

The cyber forum enabled the reporters working in many countries to collaborate, despite being separated by distance and time zones. Deputy director of the ICIJ Marina Walker Guevara said the forum was the closest they had experienced to a truly global virtual newsroom in which reporters could help one another.

Journalists shared interview transcripts, photos and confidential material, knowing that they could trust their colleagues within the network. By October the group had grown to more than 80 journalists working for dozens of different and, sometimes, competing media organisations.[12] Reporters working on the project, and the media organisations they represented, were required to agree in writing that they would not share the data files with third parties, that they would respect the story embargoes and that they would be team players.[13]

Verification of the identities of persons of interest (political leaders, military commanders, business leaders and the newly emerging Chinese generation of princelings who were related to the current and former Communist Party elders) was complicated by variations in the English spellings of names translated from Chinese characters. The identities were painstakingly clarified by a reporter in Spain who cross-referenced the lists of notable Chinese against the names of offshore clients listed in the ICIJ's database. Identities were confirmed by cross-referencing residential addresses and ID numbers where possible. Some individual identities that could not be confirmed had to be omitted from the investigation.[14]

The rollout of the news coverage was collaborative and simultaneous in order to avoid tipping off any investigation targets. The reporters agreed on a strict embargo and Secrecy for Sale articles were published in dozens of countries simultaneously with an agreed publication date of 3 April 2013 set months ahead of the publication. This enabled media outlets such as television (which has much slower production times) to gather, edit and check their work in readiness to break a major global news story. The coverage exposed international tax evasion on a massive scale in Canada, China, France, India, Israel, Russia, South Korea and the UK.[15] A result of the global coverage was that tax havens were placed on the agenda of the G20 in November 2014 in Brisbane resulting in a global political focus on the issue and new legislation in many countries. The subsequent investigations will be explored in more detail later in the book.

Awards

Gerard Ryle was awarded the Walkley Foundation's leadership award in Australia in 2014 for his coordinating role in the Secrecy for Sale investigation. The coverage also won dozens of other media awards around the globe.[16]

Journalism and Web based communications

In each of the above investigations, Web based communications were vital to the success of the coverage. Each of the investigations would have been far more difficult, much slower and more expensive – or possibly been abandoned as too costly to undertake – but for the digital connections made and the ease and speed of secure communication. The reporters were able to build a trusting rapport with news sources in their own community or across the globe; stored data was searched and retrieved from anywhere; archives were miniaturised into USB sticks or hard drives for ease of transport; sources were anonymised where necessary; public awareness was raised leading to behavioural change and laws were amended leading to improved legislation and enforcement of laws in many countries.

Data storage, miniaturisation and retention

As we have seen in the previous investigations, the storage of online data that is easily retrievable via plain language search terms provides public access to documents and news articles long after they are written. The longevity of online news text, audio and video means news and current affairs content might usefully be conceptualised as history in the making. News content may be the means by which news sources find reporters who have already written about a specific topic or event. News content thus has the potential to become, in effect, a part of the network with which interested reporters and members of the public can interact around an issue or topic.

The miniaturisation of data storage also means that very large volumes of documents can be stored digitally on small devices such as USB sticks. Large amounts of data can be downloaded, stored and removed from a relatively secure office or business environment by potential whistleblowers. The ICIJ tax haven investigation, for example, began with a whistleblower giving 2.5 million leaked offshore financial records to one reporter who, himself, was able to create a network of reporters which was able to investigate the links between the data and powerful and wealthy individuals.

Building trust

In each investigation, the reporters established trust between each other and with their news sources. ICIJ deputy director Marina Walker Guevara observed the high degree of trust between reporters who were usually rivals and commented that this trust was *even more important* than the collaborative tools and the technology being used for the global investigation. "Beyond the collaboration tools and the technology we used, we believe it was the human relationships – between coordinators and reporters and among reporters in the field – that served us best," she said.[17] The trust between the reporters enabled them to agree to set a joint publication date five months in the future.

During the ICIJ's China investigation, Chinese reporters working on the project were warned by Chinese Government officials to stop their investigations. The reporters in China withdrew from the investigation for fear of being jailed but ICIJ reporters who were outside China were able to continue the project. Had there been no collaboration, the Chinese section of the investigation could not have continued. The ICIJ conducted one of the largest public participation projects using its database of more than 37,000 high-wealth individuals in China, Taiwan and Hong Kong. In January 2015, the networks of more than 37,000 people in China, Taiwan and Hong Kong were released online by the ICIJ.[18] The database was released to the public and people were invited to comb the database to provide information to the reporters to enable them to further investigate links between China's elites who were using tax havens.[19]

Investigative uses of Web based communication technologies

Web based communication technologies including email, GPS, encrypted cyber forums, video conferencing platforms such as Skype, Zoom and Microsoft teams have become extremely useful, if not vital, for journalistic investigations. Their main functions include accessing archived evidence, obtaining physical evidence, protecting source identities and enabling public participation in journalistic investigations, exemplified by the case studies in this chapter.

Accessing archived evidence

Digital news archives and digital document archives of all kinds that are easily searchable online are a revolutionary change from analogue document searches that were geospatially limited and required substantial time to search, often rendering the search slow and cumbersome and therefore unviable. Custodians of analogue documents who could search their physical archives are also often controlled; so the seeking of permission to search may have alerted governments or organisations that searches were underway.

Obtaining physical evidence

Physical evidence may be critical to verifying facts that form the basis of an investigative story. Physical evidence may also be used to disprove allegations. In the *Concrete Creek* investigation by the *Newcastle Herald*, physical evidence in the form of photographs, videos and logged GPS positions verified that verbal claims by a mining company minimising the severity and extent of environmental damage were false. Gathering the physical evidence required shoe leather journalism guided by GPS tracking and re-tracking to verify the extent of damage in a conservation area.

Protecting source identities

Whistleblowers are people with inside knowledge of a topic, organisation or person, who are willing to share their information but who may require anonymity. Digitisation of communication has meant that journalists who have to protect a source need to ensure the whistleblower cannot be identified or traced. Lower-level precautions that can be taken include using password-protected Voice over the Internet Protocol (VoIP) software rather than landline or mobile phones. Some journalists use personal telephones rather than work telephones to better protect the identity of their sources (Meldrum-Hanna 2015). Investigative reporters also strive to protect their sources by finding ways to communicate without leaving metadata trails that risk exposing vulnerable sources. One reporter told me that:

> The ability to trace information to a source is frightening. I am constantly shocked by how people can do it. Vigilance is always needed in those cases. I think there are ways around [being traced]. I like to think that the ability to protect sources is just a little bit ahead of the ability to track them down. You just have to be careful and try to protect sources well.

Specialist organisations have produced practical guides to online safety for reporters including Reporters without Borders, Freedom of the Press Foundation and Digital Defenders Partnership.[20] A global reference guide for secure VoIP services is available at Voip-info.org.

Using analogue forms of data such as photocopied documents is not always a solution to protect sources because photocopiers can store data about the use of the machine. The usage can be traced using tracking software to find out where a particular document was photocopied.

> Even if sources photocopy information and then send it to you, there is a trace, in a photocopy machine somewhere, that they did that. And I think as soon as things are leaked, government departments and organisations can quickly put tracking software on and find out where the leak came from.

Laws governing the storage of metadata and access to stored metadata in any jurisdiction in which a reporter intends to work should be researched and understood before beginning an investigation. In Australia, for example, the Telecommunications (Interception and Access)

Amendment (Data Retention) Act 2015 requires communications carriers to keep metadata for two years.

Enabling public participation in journalistic investigations

Investigative stories of all kinds can be enhanced by public participation. Citizen participation in breaking news stories has increased, especially of major news and news events from conflict zones (Glaser 2012; Hyun 2009; Goode 2009). News outlets have invited citizen participation in large-scale investigative journalism projects that have resulted in greater public accountability of businesses and enhanced agency of individuals. For example, Tanja Aitamurto of Finland examined seven investigations in which the reporters crowd-sourced readers to report on national topics including mortgage interest rates in Sweden, gender inequalities in maths and science education, the effectiveness of government foreign aid programmes and the quality of aged care services. Reader engagement in some of the projects was very high with, for example, 40,000 readers disclosing the interest rates they were paying on their mortgage. The interest rate data was mapped and indexed by bank, postcode and the length of the loan, provoking a national debate (Aitamurto 2014).

Political events are also more accessible to the public than ever before (McNair 2014). There has been a dramatic increase since the onset of the COVID-19 pandemic by political leaders and government health officers in livestreaming media conferences directly and immediately to the public (Kapitan 2020). This trend may well continue after the pandemic, especially by naturally capable communicators.

Risks of using Web based communications

In addition to benefits, Web based communication also has inherent risks. These include risks to news sources and the emergent risk of *dis*connection.

Risks to news sources

Reporters working on some of the most controversial and sensitive investigations in this book decided they could not risk using Web based communications because of the fragile health and safety risks to their news sources. *Foreign Correspondent* producer Vivien Altman had to avoid communicating with news sources by email or by phone because of the risks to news sources.

During the course of *Prisoner X* we did become very careful. We realised, for example, that sending emails to Israel was risky, speaking to Israel on the phone was not a good idea. There were all sorts of things that made it quite difficult to do the story. But we had to take into account that it wasn't us who were going to have a problem, it was people on the other end who were going to have a problem.

The reporting team minimised risk by keeping the content of their emails as benign as possible.

Risk of disconnection

Foreign correspondent Michael Bachelard relies so heavily on internet connection that he sees the main risk in Web based communications as *disconnection* from the internet. He said:

> The main risk for me, in Indonesia particularly, is that I rely on [the internet] so profoundly, and so does my office, that if you do not have access to the internet the whole thing grinds to a halt very quickly.

Michael mitigated this risk by having multiple ways of connecting to the internet, especially when he is travelling, not only to follow a breaking story but also to file his copy.

> In my little bag of tricks, I have three different ways to connect to the Net. But if they all fail, which they did one time, when I was in Kalimantan, trying to write a very timely story about a nuance of the then-breaking Schapelle Corby story. I could write the story, but I could not get it through. So in the end I had to beg at the offices of one of the airline people, 'Can I plug into your wireless?' So the main risk for me is that negative risk.

Reporters now rely so heavily on the internet for their daily work that the risk of a major internet crash in a region or country would significantly jeopardise news production and distribution. In addition, the redundancy of copy takers and switchboard operators means there is no fall-back analogue method. Further research into the mechanisms being used by other reporters in transnational and global investigations has the potential to add to the emerging scholarship in this field and to the changing skill set required by reporters entering the journalism industry.

Digital hyper-connectivity

Web based communication technologies such as email and Skype have been readily adopted into the work routines of investigative journalists because of the obvious advantages they offer. Web based communication technologies help to overcome geographic and temporal barriers to communication. They are cheap to use, flexible and adaptable and quickly became ubiquitous as networks, allowing reporters to keep contemporaneous records that could easily be archived. Reporters who worked as foreign correspondents and adopted Skype technology primarily to save on private telephone bills, discovered they could use Skype in their work to interview news sources overseas. This had the effect of globalising their potential field of news contacts and enabling them to develop a more global view of their stories. The discovery that they could achieve face-to-face communication cheaper, faster and more easily than by using previous technologies such as telephones or satellite phones expanded the range of stories they could research and write. The case studies in this chapter indicate that it is possible to cover sensitive and controversial issues more comprehensively, more cost-effectively and more quickly using Web based communication technologies that are as simple as email, Skype and GPS. The reporters were able to prove allegations by gathering timely, accurate information more quickly than was ever possible before the digital age and to use it to create public sphere journalism that created meaningful social and political change.

The three investigations in this chapter could have been conducted without the use of Web based technologies; however, the use of this technology enabled the reporters to obtain incontrovertible evidence to prove the true extent of the environmental damage from mining in a particular context. So, although the mining company had minimised the damage and the government had not asked for repairs to be carried out, the investigation and media exposure led to both the company and the government being called to account. The Bangladesh factory collapse would have been reported – much as the previous factory collapses and worker deaths had been reported – without yielding lasting change; however the collaboration between reporters inside and outside the country and the pressure brought to bear by overseas consumers of the products led to better enforcement of building codes to reduce the risk of future building collapses and improved wages for workers. The tax haven investigation may have been reported partially in some countries given a major investment of time and effort, but it is unlikely that global attention would have been focused on the problem had it not been for this collaboration. The cyber forum and the global collaboration focused world attention on the injustice of tax havens and yielded collaboration of the G20 leaders to pass legislation in many countries to prevent money laundering and tax evasion.

The following two chapters focus on the two remaining aspects of investigative journalism that have the potential to strengthen the global fourth estate: reporter collaboration and media outlet collaboration.

Notes

1 *Telegraph.* 2007. "The Very Reverend Robert Waddington." London: Telegraph Media Group Limited, 23 March 2007; *The Times.* 2007. "The Very Reverend Robert Waddington." London, News UK: *The Times.* 23 March 2007; and David Guide. 2007. "Robert Waddington." Cumbria, Newsquest: *News & Star.* 13 April 2007.

2 *The Times.* 2007. "The Very Reverend Robert Waddington." London, News UK: *The Times.* 23 March 2007.

3 Bellingcat. 2020. https://www.bellingcat.com.

4 D. Page. 2013. "Mine subsidence devastates Sugarloaf conservation area." Newcastle NSW, Newcastle Newspapers: *Newcastle Herald*, 27 August 2013.

5 D. Page 2013. "Sugarloaf coalmine subsidence repair disaster." Newcastle NSW, Newcastle Newspapers: *Newcastle Herald*, 28 August 2013.

6 Donna Page, Darren Pateman and Matt Carr. PhD Interviews. 2014.

7 B. Doherty and S. Whyte. 2013. "Don't abandon us: Bangladeshis." *The Sydney Morning Herald*, 24 June 2013. B. Doherty. 2013. "Right now we have nothing." *The Sydney Morning Herald*, 24 June 2013; B. Doherty and S. Whyte. 2013. "Kmart to reveal global factory locations." *The Sydney Morning Herald.* 10 July 2013.

8 Gerard Ryle. 2013a. "How ICIJ chose our offshore reporting partners." 10 April 2013. www.icij.org/blog/2013/04/how-icij-chose-our-reporting-partners.

9 Marina Walker Guevara. 2014a. "How we did Offshore Leaks China." ICIJ Blog, 21 January 2014. www.icij.org/blog/2014/01/how-we-did-offshore-leaks-china.

10 Gerard Ryle, Marina Walker Guevara, Michael Hudson, Nicky Hager, Duncan Campbell and Stefan Candea. 2013. "Secrecy for sale: inside the global offshore money maze." https://cloudfront-files-1.publicintegrity.org.

11 Marina Walker Guevara. 2014. "Luxembourg leaks: a case study in collaborative journalism." ICIJ: *The Global Muckraker*, 6 November 2014.

12 Ibid.

13 Marina Walker Guevara 2013. "How we all survived likely the largest collaboration in journalism history." ICIJ: *The Global Muckraker.* 12 April 2013.

14 Marina Walker Guevara. 2014. "How we did Offshore Leaks China." ICIJ Blog, 21 January 2014. www.icij.org/blog/2014/01/how-we-did-offshore-leaks-china.

15 ICIJ. 2012. "Secrecy for sale: inside the global offshore money maze." www.icij.org/offshore.

16 The Centre for Public Integrity. Awards. https://publicintegrity.org/about/awards.

17 Marina Walker Guevara. 2013. "How we all survived likely the largest colla-boration in journalism history." ICIJ: *The Global Muckraker.* 12 April 2013.
18 Marina Walker Guevara. 2014. "How we did Offshore Leaks China." ICIJ Blog, 21 January 2014. www.icij.org.
19 Gerard Ryle. 2013. "How ICIJ chose our offshore reporting partners." www.icij.org/blog.
20 Secure VoIP Service Providers. https://www.voip-info.org.

6 Reporter collaboration

Many investigative reporters are classic lone wolves, working in isolation and extremely protective of their work.[1]

Collaboration by work colleagues is well recognised in many fields, such as in scientific and medical research, industry, artistic endeavours, political movements and many other sectors of human activity as a means to achieve synergistic results (Castells 2009). The opposite has tended to apply in investigative journalism. The professional identity of investigative journalists has rested to a significant degree on their ability to work independently, to develop trusted contacts inside organisations and government departments, to be able to verify facts quickly and to have the courage to challenge authority in the public sphere, in the interests of democracy. Collaboration is emerging as a *method* in the digital age for undertaking investigative reporting that synergises the investigation by co-opting colleagues with specific contacts, skills and access to information or who live in different locations.

Collaboration is a partnership arrangement in which a reporter works with one or more trusted colleagues, sharing elements of their investigative workload such as their story lead, contacts or investigatory and writing tasks. Just as some reporters are discovering the power of networking via social media and Web based communication technologies, they are also discovering the power of working in an exclusive network with one or more colleagues. The collaborating reporters might be located in the same media outlet; or might work for the same media company but in different offices or different states or countries; or they might work for rival media outlets in the same country or in different countries. The news stories that result from the collaboration may be published in one publication under shared by-lines; or each reporter may write or produce their own coverage from the findings of the collaborative investigation.

DOI: 10.4324/9781003139980-6

As my investigation into Robert Waddington's offending in Australia and Britain progressed and I had drafted the main feature story, I needed a national media outlet to publish it in the UK and, hopefully, a national media outlet to publish it in Australia as well. I spoke to long-time colleague Michael McKenna at *The Australian*. He was interested in the potential of the story as an international story as well as an Australian national story. In an interview with Michael after the investigation was completed, he explained his reasons for agreeing to the collaboration. First, the two initial news sources who were bringing the child sexual abuse allegations were willing to be tested; secondly, the story highlighted how offenders could move between countries; thirdly, the story demonstrated how international institutions could easily deny allegations of abuse; and, finally, because enablers of the offender had not yet been held to account for facilitating ongoing abuse of children.

Michael and I agreed that we needed to also collaborate with a reporter in the UK to save us having either to work at a distance, or to spend the time and cost of travelling to the UK, which was not viable. We wanted to work with someone in a News Corp publication if possible, rather than across media companies. News Corp's national daily newspaper in the UK, *The Times,* was our first preference. I searched for some background on the crime editor, Sean O'Neill, read some of his stories and his evidence to the Leveson Inquiry. It seemed that reporters had not collaborated between the two newspapers before, but Michael McKenna was confident of being able to negotiate a one-off informal collaboration directly with Sean who could persuade his editor to come on board. By early May 2013, both Eli and Bim were emotionally robust enough to be interviewed and were determined that they would waive their right to anonymity and be named. Both men had spent some months contemplating that the story could attract significant media coverage in both countries because it spanned the globe and because Waddington was one of the most high-ranking Anglican clergy to be exposed as a child sex offender. Michael flew to north Queensland to interview Bim. On the same day, Sean travelled by train to Northamptonshire to interview Eli.

Eli Ward asked me to be present via Skype during his interview with Sean O'Neill. This meant I was able to send documents Sean asked for, so he could verify the information about the allegations. Eli's plans to be identified were almost de-railed because on the morning of the interview Eli heard that his nephew had died. Due to the shock of this death, Eli Ward's lawyer believed Eli should remain anonymous in all media coverage. However, Eli Ward was determined – as he had been over the previous months – that his childhood photo must be published in order to try to make contact with the victim in the additional photograph that he had seen in the offender's study. The lawyer's caution was noted but not heeded. Eli Ward was determined he wanted to be named and identified in the coverage and Sean O'Neill agreed to fulfil his wish. News copy was written for *The Australian* and *The Times* and the package of news and feature stories was sent for legal clearance.

Once the first stories were published in Australia and the UK, the speed of the investigation ramped up substantially. In each 24 hours, the time zone difference of 10 hours between the Australian east coast and London meant that, as a team, we were working on the story almost 24 hours a day, sending each other updates and leads to follow up. The stories being published also attracted reader comments to the newspapers' websites and extensive comment on social media platforms. Reader response in both countries led to new breaks in the story almost every day.[2] While it was foreseeable that there would be more victims of abuse by Waddington, it was optimistic to hope they might respond during a blaze of media coverage, especially given the distressing nature of the topic for victims. Despite knowing they would be stepping into a media spotlight, more victims did make contact directly with one of our team of reporters in either Australia or the UK.

The following case studies of collaborations highlight the increased speed and political influence that media coverage can achieve when a lone reporter with a story lead invites trusted colleagues into a collaboration.

Case study 10: *Prisoner X*

Four Corners reporter Trevor Bormann was in Israel conducting an interview and was called into another room and given a story lead by an unknown person. The person said, "Look, I can't do this, but it's important. I can only give you this much detail, because that's all I know." The details were sketchy but involved a young man from Australia who had gone to Israel and allegedly committed suicide in a suicide-proof cell in a jail under mysterious circumstances. Media reporting of the case had been banned in Israel due to it being declared a matter of national security.[3] Trevor needed help to verify the facts. He needed someone with strong connections in the Jewish community in Australia who might be able to identify the man who he knew only as Prisoner X. Once back in Australia, he asked one of his colleagues, Vivien Altman, who had some contacts in the Jewish community, to collaborate with him. He handed over the sketchy details he had and asked for her help. The details handed on to Vivien Altman were:

> There is a young man who came to Israel who we think is from
> Australia and who obviously got himself into a mess ... I think he
> did actually say he was working for Mossad. '[He] got married,
> got himself into trouble and was put in jail and then died under
> mysterious circumstances.'

There was no other information. It was an intriguing story lead about a
potential spy from Australia working for Mossad – and who was now dead.

Vivien dialled a few numbers, including a former journalist colleague, giving the few details she had and asking for information. One of
her contacts said he would make some calls and call her back the next
day if he found anything. Surprisingly, he called back within half an hour
and was able to tell Vivien about an Australian who had died in Israel
who might be their Prisoner X. Ben Zygier, 34, was a young Australian
lawyer who had travelled to Israel, allegedly worked for Mossad and died
in jail. Vivien was very shocked because she had known Ben Zygier's
family very well many years before. "My ex-boyfriend had actually lived
at the parents' house, so I used to spend a lot of time at Ben's parents'
house," she said.

Whilst the mystery of the identity of Prisoner X was solved extraordinarily quickly, knowing the identity of Prisoner X plunged Vivien
into an ethical dilemma because the parents of Prisoner X did not
want any news coverage about their son's plight due to their fears for
the safety of anyone connected with him.

> [The mother] was very upset. Her voice was shaking and she was
> terribly upset. I think one of the things was (remember there was a
> gag order on this story in Israel) she was genuinely scared. I was
> taken aback by this very strong reaction. After that, of course, I
> knew a lot of people who knew them, so what I did was started
> contacting people and tried to find out more.

Vivien was not sure how to protect the initial news source in Israel;
how to minimise the physical risks to other potential news sources in
Israel; how to safely report a story on which a foreign government had
issued a gag order; and how to resolve whether to cover the story at
all – given the fear of the family of the central character in the story
and their opposition to coverage.

With no cooperation from the family, Vivien Altman decided to go
to Melbourne and spoke to friends of Zygier, who were willing to be
interviewed. She resolved that the public interest in finding out why an
Australian citizen had died in an Israeli jail took precedence over her

loyalty to a family she had known – but not seen again – since her teenage years.

> I had not seen them for a very long time. How can I put it? They were people that I knew in the 1970s. I had stayed in their house, and I had known them well. But fast forward, I had not actually seen them since then. We are talking about 2013. So how did I justify it? Well, I thought it was important in the public interest. I really did. I thought it was important journalistically. I was very concerned about the parents. Very concerned, and in fact I thought there were a lot of ethical questions because I knew that very strongly, they did not want the story broadcast. And I knew that if we ever got the story to air – because at that stage it was early days – that it would really upset them.

Vivien Altman's personal connection with Ben Zygier's family and friends meant that the reporters were able to find contacts who gave them information on the record that established Ben Zygier's good character. "It was a very sad story," Vivien Altman said.

> There was nothing redemptive about it. He was just this young, idealistic man who had gone to Israel, and one way or another he had worked as a lawyer and then was recruited, and got himself into this thing and got deeper and deeper and made some very bad decisions and got himself into a terrible mess. A really serious mess. And he was facing a pretty bleak future away from his family. He was to all intents and purposes a very nice, sensitive young man. So it was just very sad.

Despite all the difficulties, the story was produced and broadcast. Ben Zygier's family never changed their initial perspective. "To the end they were resolute. Very angry and very upset, and that hasn't changed to this day." Vivien Altman's quandary is far from unique. Her courage in continuing on with the story which eventually honoured Ben Zygier's memory is testament to her commitment to exposing the truth no matter how uncomfortable that truth, or the process by which it is revealed.

Once the *Prisoner X* investigation was broadcast in Australia, the *Four Corners* reporters were contacted by many overseas reporters who shared information that helped to advance the story. Journalists in other countries collaborated, leading to further revelations in both Australian and overseas media. Vivien Altman and Trevor Bormann shared unpublished information with reporters in other countries to help them all advance the story, especially in Israel. "I think it had a huge reaction from Israel. Some of it was social media, but some of it was just people ringing," Vivien Altman said.

> The phone just rang and rang and rang with people from Israel who were trying to cover it in Israel and find out what was going on in Australia. And some of that was through social media but more of it was just journalists trying to follow me and trying to contact me and they wanted to contact other people in Australia. So there was a sharing of information as well because there was a sense of, look, this is a story where I might be able to give information, and they might be able to give information to me. Because it was a story that had global ramifications – it affected more than one country.

In this story, collaboration between reporters was vital to verify and break the story but was also vital in advancing the story in Israel. The combination of techniques yielded an important international story emanating from Australia that called a foreign government to account for the death of an Australian prisoner.

Award

The *Prisoner X* programmes won the Walkley Award for All Media Investigative Journalism and another for TV/AV Weekly Current Affairs.[4] The stories were also recognised for the excellence of the investigation winning a television Logie and a Silver World Medal for Best Investigative Report at the New York Film Festival.

Case study 11: *Secret tapes*

A bundle of covertly recorded tapes was handed by a whistleblower to James Campbell, the state politics editor for the *Herald Sun* and the *Sunday Herald Sun* in 2013. The four hours of revelations concerning police and senior government officials were explosive. Careful verification of the tapes was conducted. Legal opinion was sought as to whether the contents could be published. Once clearance was given, transcriptions were made and checked. The next task was to select the strongest news angles in discussion with editors and chiefs of staff. "We knew the tapes were dynamite. Once we had a legal opinion that we could publish them, we then were transcribing them," he said. Mr Campbell chose to invite his colleagues to collaborate and shared the tapes with four colleagues to speed up the process of transcribing them. Matt Johnson, Michelle Ainsworth, Annika Smethurst and Mitchell Toy met at an off-site location and worked there to protect the confidentiality of the material from any risk of leakage. James Campbell said:

> It took several days and the transcriptions had to be verified by the people listening to them. There were certain people whose names we redacted because they weren't material to it. Then I worked with editors and chiefs of staff on what we thought the best news lines were out of them.

As the transcriptions of each tape were completed, James wrote the first group of stories. News editors at the *Herald Sun* then discussed how to achieve the greatest political impact with the story – whether to break the story sequentially over several days or to take the "nuclear option" of publishing all the news reports and audio on the same day. The team then worked together on follow up stories and Mitchell Toy edited the audio recordings for the newspaper's website so that readers could listen to sections of the audio for themselves. "After questioning whether to roll the story out over several days, the newspaper decided on the big bang approach which resulted in Victorian Premier Ted Baillieu resigning the same day," Campbell said. The story splashed on 4 March 2013, exposing secret dealings, payments and information that contradicted public statements by the Premier.[5] Reflecting on the choice of the "nuclear option," Mr Campbell said this had delivered maximum impact. He added:

> The decision was influenced by which approach might be more likely to persuade other media to follow the story. We had people going to the [web]site and listening to the tapes. We had thousands of people who listened to all of them – the whole thing. Many thousands listened to the edited highlights.

The story broke as a five-page exposé with online links to the audio of the secret tapes.

Award

James Campbell won the 2013 Walkley Award for All Media Scoop of the Year for his investigation into secret Liberal Party interference in the police command crisis in Victoria.

Collaboration

For several of the reporters included in this study, collaboration was already a preferred and routine way of working. For others, collaboration was accidental, emerging from a desperate need, or arose in a novel manner. The reasons for collaborating cited here include a need to improve personal safety; speeding up an investigation to compete with rival news outlets; saving time and travel costs; or gaining access to particular contacts. The dynamics of domestic newsgathering are also being changed by technologies that enable online collaboration, creating what journalist Sarah Whyte describes as a hyper-reality.

> It is very quick and easy. It's convenient in gathering facts and figures. You are working in a hyper-reality. In the Press Gallery you are working in that anyway. It is very collective, if you miss something you are able to find someone else who has got it on Twitter. I just use the hashtag to look it up.

Collaboration between reporters and between media outlets is beginning to emerge as an important method of carrying out routine journalism in the networked media environment.

There are significant benefits for reporters who are willing to collaborate with other reporters, whether in different media organisations, states or countries, which enables more complex stories to be researched and published. The power of collaboration is underlined by the fact that almost all of the finalists and winners of the hotly contested All Media sections of the 2013 Walkley Awards that pit newspaper, radio, television and online reporting against each other were *collaborations* of two or more reporters, usually working with one or more technical colleagues. Most of the investigative stories in this book were facilitated by collaborations between two or more journalists. In some investigations the collaboration was key, such as in *Prisoner X* and the *Secret tapes* bombshell, while in other investigations collaboration assisted significantly, such as in *Shine the light*, *Bangladesh factory collapse*, *Firestorm*, *Concrete Creek* and the *Tax haven investigation*.

Collaboration can be a vital ingredient in finding, verifying or publishing an investigative story despite the hyper-connectivity of the digitised world. Collaboration helps to counteract the lack of funds available for staff, travel and other costs. So, despite the financial pressures, public sphere journalism produced by collaborating journalists working within a media organisation, across states, across countries or in cooperation with reporters in several different states or countries is able to call powerful organisations and governments to account. The paradigm of the lone wolf investigative reporter is waning. While it may still be possible to produce investigative journalism as an individual reporter, the benefits of collaboration in the digital age give journalists who are willing to work with others an edge over those who restrict themselves to working alone.

Some groups of collaborating reporters have been formed to undertake investigations that involve the increasing connectedness of power, influence and corruption. The Global Environmental Journalism Initiative (GEJI), for example, is a consortium of academics and student reporters from nine tertiary institutions in Europe and Australia (Bacon 2011). Initial GEJI projects have included coverage of issues such as renewable energy, plastic bag usage and climate change. Bacon's recognition of the need for a global perspective on such topics echoes Steven Ward's call for a radical rethinking of journalism as a responsible global citizen when he wrote that "Journalists' primary allegiance is to truthful, independent informing of a global humanity" (Ward 2005, 328). Project Censored, another academic-student collaboration that started in Canada and the US in the 1970s to report under-covered or censored stories, has grown into a network of hundreds of academics with thousands of students from tertiary journalism institutions (Bacon 2011). Students with digital knowledge and skills who graduate and move into the profession will provide an important source of skilled practitioners who could be expected to thrive in the network society and to have an increasingly global outlook.

But some experienced investigative reporters are likely to have worked independently for most of their career. Foreign correspondent Michael Bachelard, for example, prefers to work alone even though he recognises the benefits of collaboration:

> I'm a lone wolf by nature as well as by circumstance. I wouldn't seek out anyone else to share the story with. I would generally try and do it myself. I often regard my lone-wolfness as a handicap, not as an advantage. I look at the collaboration that Nick McKenzie has with Richard Baker. I think that's done them both a lot of good.

Reasons for collaboration

Despite a general reluctance to collaborate, fear and resistance were overcome by the reporters in this research by their dedication to their task and the practical necessities such as improving physical safety, the need for particular skills or experience, the lack of funding available for domestic or international travel, the need for particular news contacts, the need to speed up an urgent investigation and the financial need to pool data to save expenses. Each of these is now addressed in turn.

Safety

Reporters may collaborate in an attempt to improve their physical safety. Foreign correspondents who work in conflict zones or wars are more at risk if they travel alone than if they are with other reporters. Journalists who meet others on the front lines, often work together to improve their personal protection, especially if their coverage is destined for media outlets in different countries which are therefore competing in different media markets from each other. Michael Bachelard observed that

> people in war zones collaborate for security, essentially. [One says] 'I don't want to travel in here alone. Let's get a group of us and we'll go together.' But they tend to be non-competing. So, an Australian news organisation would go together with someone from the BBC, or another outlet.

Pooling skills

Operating in a multimedia environment requires journalists to have a growing range of technical skills. Collaboration between reporters who have complementary skills in interviewing, audio and video can enhance the production of the multimedia media package, especially when there is a limited timeframe for gathering information and audio and video footage as well as writing and editing. Combinations of reporters with photographers, videographers and website builders are making coverage possible which previously was prohibitively expensive in time and/or money. One reporter observed the synergies between the digital native generation and a more experienced reporter on the staff who swapped social media help in exchange for assistance with interviewing and writing techniques.

Financial/economic benefits

Collaboration provides a technique for reporters to save significant travel expenses and associated costs. Newspapers in Australia which have foreign correspondents are more frequently calling on their overseas staff members to follow up story leads or verify information in collaboration with their reporters in Australia.

Pooling contacts

In Castells' network society, one's presence in, or absence from, the network is of critical importance. Investigative journalists who each have connection with the network and who pool their connections can vastly increase their overall connectedness. Information gleaned from online or face-to-face interviews can be used to launch additional online searches or precipitate further interviews until the information is verified or disproven. For example, *The Age's* investigative duo Richard Baker and Nick McKenzie broke their Essendon drug scandal series by following leads from face-to-face interviews with known or unknown contacts who were whistleblowers. Richard Baker described this process:

> You get a bit of information, but then you use your existing contacts, and this is why working in combination works together, because you broaden that field of people that you know. So, you reach out, you build upon that initial bit of information. You try and confirm it and learn more through various channels. It's not just one person comes and gives you the whole box and dice.

In addition, people in sensitive positions need to be protected from being identified as sources.

Saving investigation time

The time taken to research and verify the facts in an investigation can be prohibitively costly: saving time also saves money. The quicker a lead can be either discarded or verified, the better. Facts which cannot be verified, although potentially true, cannot be published because of the legal risks. If collaboration enables facts and associations to be verified more quickly, then a story is more likely to eventuate for the investment of time made by the media company and the reporter. In this process, trust between the reporters is vital to the success of the investigation. In the *Prisoner X* investigation, for example, the trust between colleagues meant the reporter who had been given the story lead was willing to share the lead in the hope of his colleague being able to find a news source – which happened very quickly. For reporters who regularly work in collaboration, their established trust allows them to verify or discard potential leads more quickly, as Richard Baker explained: "If you combine your research, you can get out and get a greater understanding of what is there and that is far quicker than if you do it on your own." Although investigative reporting usually operates outside the 24/7 news cycle, the speed of the investigation can sometimes be vital to its success.

Pooling data

The cost of data access can be a barrier to reporting on government activity because Right to Information (RTI) applications can be costly. Media outlets can maximise the benefit of paying for RTI applications by having reporters collaborating to mine the data for potential stories. Evidence from *Newcastle Herald* reporter Matt Carr indicates news outlets are willing to finance access to government data even when it is not clear what editorial outcomes are likely to emerge. *Newcastle Herald* reporters routinely work together on government data sets. "They do not necessarily know what the lead is, but they are just trying to trawl through the data to get the picture," Carr said. A similar process could be conducted between non-competitive media outlets covering different readerships and therefore enabling coverage of public sphere issues without creating conflict or competition between media outlets.

The examples given above show reporters are successfully collaborating to improve personal safety, to pool their skills, to pool contacts, to save travel time and costs and to save investigation time. The outstanding results of these collaborations indicate that collaboration is a very useful technique for reporting in the digital age. Reporters who are also able to persuade their media organisations to collaborate to investigate, verify and publish stories can gain enormous additional advantages, as the next chapter will show.

Notes

1 Marina Walker Guevara. 2013. "How we all survived likely the largest collaboration in journalism history." ICIJ: *The Global Muckraker*. 12 April 2013.
2 The story was published by mainstream newspaper, radio, television and online media outlets and church media in the UK, the US, France, Australia and other countries.
3 Vivien Altman. 2013. "Prisoner X – the Australian connection." Australia: *Four Corners*. ABC Television. 12 February 2013.
4 Vivien Altman. 2013. "Prisoner X – The Australian Connection." Australia: *Four Corners*. ABC Television. 12 February 2013.
5 James Campbell. 2013. "Secret tapes bombshell." *Herald Sun*. 4 March 2013. https://www.melbournepressclub.com.

7 Media outlet collaboration

It was a risky approach, but we did not see any other way around it.[1]

The jealousy with which reporters guard their story leads is matched only by the jealousy with which media outlets guard their exclusive stories. Until recently, sharing exclusive stories has been very unusual but digital disruption has forged change, despite the general reluctance of the industry. Collaboration between media outlets is emerging as a way for different media, for example newspapers and television, to share the cost and workload of investigations and to maximise their audience and thus enhance the political impact of the story. When I approached the crime editor of *The Times* in London with a story lead and told him I was already working with the political editor at *The Australian* but we'd both like to work with *The Times*, Sean O'Neill was initially sceptical that his newspaper would agree. However, he loved the story idea and wanted to be involved. The practicalities were that the story had a necessary Australian component that he needed but could not get alone. The story also had an English component that we could not achieve without his help. In practical terms, a media outlet collaboration was the answer but even though both papers are owned by NewsCorp it had never been done to his knowledge. Sean offered to speak to his managers to seek their agreement.

Collaboration between our mastheads in different countries promised to vastly reduce editorial costs by removing the cost of international travel for reporters in both countries: the Waddington investigation would probably not have been possible without such collaboration and savings.

Even if the Australian reporters had been funded to go to the UK, it would have been difficult to gain access to the key sources. Michael McKenna said:

DOI: 10.4324/9781003139980-7

I don't think that I would get anywhere close to Lord David Hope of Thornes or the English hierarchy of that institution even if I had gone over there for a month or two, or if you had come over with me. It would have cost us a lot of money and I don't think we would have advanced it as far. So that is how I was able to convince the newspaper that it was time to do a collaboration.

This factor became the key reason why *The Australian* newspaper agreed to share an exclusive story with *The Times* and risk a collaboration.

Another significant reason for *The Australian* inviting *The Times* to collaborate was the need to have a British newspaper challenging the Church of England *in England*. Michael McKenna explained the reason for their reluctant agreement to collaborate:

We did not want to give a story to someone else but we both agreed that this was the way to do it. The way to confront the church was to have the institutional might of the London *Times* to take on the institutional might of the Church of England. Because even if we are a significant newspaper in this country, we could not kick the door like the London *Times*. Normally we would do that ourselves but because [the allegations] went so high within the Church of England, I knew they would not take our enquiries seriously enough if it came from a newspaper in Australia. They would have said 'oh an Australian newspaper, go away, we do not dance for this. They are not here. What would they know?' And they would have hid behind that.

Synchronous publication

An agreement was made between the reporters to have the story appear simultaneously in both countries. To achieve this, the physical newspaper story would be published on Friday morning in Australia and online in Britain at midnight on Thursday night, with *The Times* physical paper appearing 10 hours later.[2] To sweeten the deal, Michael McKenna agreed to hold an angle back in Australia so Sean could have a fresh exclusive lead that was relevant to the English end of the story. However, just before the deadline on the planned date for publication, the whole package of stories was held back due to another large breaking story in Britain that claimed the front page of *The Times* on 3 May 2013. Sean O'Neill let Michael McKenna know what was happening behind the scenes and sought his co-operation to delay the package by a week.

Despite the decision to proceed with the collaboration, both mastheads were suspicious of the other and the agreement risked breaking down if one masthead published ahead of the other. Michael McKenna also felt pressure from his newspaper managers. "There was constant pressure and fear that [*The Times*] was going to jump and break the story ahead of us and that it was going to be on my head," he said. However, the British publication was vulnerable to *The Australian* publishing unilaterally and first because the reporters in Australia had direct contact with victims in both countries, but *The Times* only had one news source in Britain. *The Times* was also vulnerable because *The Australian* had the benefit of time zones, being 10 hours ahead of London time, thus giving time for other Australian publications with British mastheads such as the *Guardian* to pick up the story in Australia, and for their correspondents in Australia to send the story to London and publish online before *The Times* could get to press with a physical paper in the UK. Michael McKenna persuaded his editor that he and Sean trusted each other and reminded the editor that the story needed strong coverage in the UK to be effective.

The success of the collaboration despite the hiccough of the one-week delay indicates the high level of trust needed – and given – between reporters collaborating on an international story of this calibre. The package was held over until the following week to target the highest publication days. The story was published simultaneously, as agreed, the following week on page one of *The Times* in London and page one of *The Australian* on 10 May 2013. Over the following weeks, months and years, more than 20 articles were published, covering the subsequent inquiry, the findings of the inquiry and the political and social impact. The coverage was politically powerful. The voices of the victims, Ward and Atkinson, who had been silenced for three decades and five decades respectively, were finally heard in the public sphere and the institution which had protected the offender was called to account. The publication was accompanied by an editorial calling for the mandatory reporting of alleged abuse by churches to the police, and led to a subsequent inquiry, admissions and reforms in the UK.[3] Eli Ward also wanted to do a television interview to maximise the chances of finding other victims of Waddington and to encourage other victims of child abuse by clergy to come forward. He chose Lucy Manning as his preferred reporter on ITV – the same reporter who had exposed the Jimmy Savile case and triggered Eli Ward's fight for justice. The morning the story was published in the UK, Eli was up early and on a train to London where he appeared in an ITV interview with Lucy Manning.[4]

Recovery and catharsis for the whistleblowers

The ability of publications on either side of the world to collaborate made it possible for isolated victims of crime in different countries to bring an international injustice to the public sphere for resolution. Without the collaboration, both news sources might have died in despair; and the institutional corruption might have continued. As the coverage was poised for publication on 3 May 2013, Eli Ward wrote that as a result of the collaborative investigation he felt hope for the first time that his future could be happy. He also had a sense of personal satisfaction that other victims might also be inspired to report abuse. Interestingly, Eli Ward used the three words "so much pain" which were eerily similar to the words John Pirona had used when he wrote his suicide note – the words that became the theme of Joanne McCarthy's coverage of paedophilia in the Newcastle Diocese. Eli described his sense of vindication to Bim in an email:

> This time last year, I didn't know my arse from my elbow. I was in a mental health home and had no idea what was happening to me. I had no idea you existed or Amanda or the others. I had been rebuilding my life every 3–4 years and going through *so much pain*. There was a huge gap in my life, unanswered questions and a gut instinct that burned with knowledge that there was something gravely wrong about my life. Now I can start to fill in the pieces about my life, understand what has happened and have started to address issues and rid myself of the people who were making my life difficult. I have learned life's hard lessons and although that was tough at first to swallow, the truth about my life is far easier to comprehend and I can compartmentalise it and move on. I can see perhaps a bright future and smatterings of happiness which I didn't see before. Going public is the least I can do to potentially unwrap the lives of others. Others like you and I.
>
> (emphasis added)

Confronting as it was for Eli Ward and Bim Atkinson to place themselves in the international media spotlight, they gained substantial validation of their plight and vindication of their allegations.

In a later email to me, Ward explained the repair he experienced due to being believed, meeting another survivor who validated his experience and seeing the power of the collaborative news coverage: "Collectively, meeting and finding you, Bim, and then obviously on to the story and everything else, has repaired me better than anything I could ever have imagined because I was no longer isolated." Mr Ward's life has stabilised, and he has a devoted partner and a delightful child – a future that he had felt no hope of achieving when I met him. In addition, he has pushed one of England's oldest and most powerful institutions towards reforms that are vital to the safety of children.

Setting a precedent

In a debrief discussion with Michael McKenna, he said he was surprised in retrospect that collaborations had not been a regular feature of investigative reporting internationally across the News Limited group of newspapers.

> It astounds me that we have not done this before. Why didn't we collaborate for instance on the World Cup soccer bribery scandals? Australia was in the most recent bribery scandal – apparently right in the guts of it. We were handing over tens of millions of dollars to grubs. *The Sunday Times* was running it. We had investigations going here. Why didn't we collaborate?

Lack of collaboration in the past appears to have been a consequence merely of a lack of initiative. "I don't think the people have really thought about it, and that is what Rupert Murdoch said to Chris Mitchell and to the editor of *The Times* in London that this should be, in his words, 'a template for future investigations.'" Despite the success of the collaboration, no formal process was apparently established to replicate the investigation procedure. However, a precedent has been set which can now be more easily followed.

> Murdoch saw it and loved it and like so many things they just moved on. But now they have a precedent, so that a London *Times* person can say 'we have done it before. We can collaborate with *The Australian*. Let's talk to the editors.'

Reform

The endemic corruption in Church institutions in both countries surrounding Waddington's offending could not have been exposed except for the collaboration of media outlets in England and Australia. The success of what was believed to be the first UK-Australia Newscorp collaboration resulted in sweeping institutional reforms. Two days after the story was published, the Archbishop of York set up an independent inquiry into Waddington. The following day the Archbishop of Canterbury promised an audit of clerical abuse cases because of the tell-tale signals of Waddington's paedophilia that were so obvious in his career progression. The initial stories resulted in two independent inquiries in the UK[5] and an inquiry in Australia through the existing Royal Commission into Institutional Reponses to Child Sexual Abuse in Australia. The collaboration produced a series of articles in the UK and Australia and led to an independent Church inquiry that substantiated the allegations, identified several other victims and found that various Church officials had protected Waddington for decades from police prosecution. The former Archbishop of York, Archbishop David Hope, was found to have failed to follow Child Protection Protocols 18 times. These failures were aggravated by the fact that Archbishop Hope had overseen the protocols as they were being written. The media outlet collaboration on a story in the UK that was researched and written in Australia led eventually to national reforms of child protection across the world and called into question the seal of the confessional that had been established in 1603 (Cahill 2014). Eight years after I met Eli Ward in a warm pub on a snowy night in Cambridge in 2012, a national British child abuse inquiry released its report on the Anglican Church, commenting in the executive summary on the attention Church leaders had paid to offenders including Waddington, instead of focusing on the risks they posed to children (Jay et al. 2020).

The collaboration also had a profound impact on the reporters involved. At the time Sean O'Neill interviewed Eli Ward in 2013, Sean was undergoing chemotherapy. Despite his illness, Sean was strongly committed to the story. When Sean announced in 2018 that he was retiring, he wrote about his career and noted that the collaboration on the Waddington investigation had given him the most personal satisfaction as a reporter.[6] Eli Ward responded in tears, that the collaboration between 'good people' had given him a new lease on life.

> Amanda has very kindly forwarded this article where you pinpointed my story as one being of the most personal satisfaction to yourself. As was my reaction then, so it was just now, having just read it. Only, however, tears of liberation and the realisation that there are true and good people on the planet.
>
> Thanks to you both, I am able to see the joys in my life, clearly, and without the clouded-ness of general life. This has given me a focus, a purpose and a reason to love life.
>
> Kindness is the greatest power we have.

This brief exchange between a news source and a reporter illuminates at the deepest human level, why investigative reporters do what they do, and the immense satisfaction there is for reporters in making a difference to people's lives.

The next two case studies trace the formation of collaborations between media outlets that have exposed very high-value national, international and global corruption.

Case study 12: *Securency*

James Shelton had been working at the Reserve Bank of Australia's currency firm Securency and had seen peculiar deals in which it appeared that overseas agents of Securency were being paid multi-million-dollar bribes to secure banknote contracts for the supply of Australian-made polymer bank notes.[7] James Shelton and another employee, Brian Hood, made complaints to their employers, to the Board of the Reserve Bank and to the police. Both men became frustrated by the lack of investigation into the allegations and eventually approached the media as a last resort. James Shelton explained in a television interview:

> The [Reserve Bank] board didn't want to know, the AFP didn't want to know, others I'd spoken to around government didn't want to know, but they did start to act when it was on the front page of the newspaper.[8]

Melbourne-based reporters Richard Baker and Nick McKenzie investigated the allegations and found after a couple of days of internet searches that some of the overseas agents had been implicated in previous corruption scandals.[9] The high value of the alleged bribes and the high level of the alleged corruption would make the story challenging to verify and publish: travelling to several countries would be costly in time and money; it would be potentially difficult to find sources who were willing to confirm the allegations and provide evidence; and it would be potentially dangerous. The reporters continued for eight months, building a network of collaborating reporters in the foreign countries where the corrupt deals were being made. The collaborative relationships established on the Securency story outlasted the investigation and have extended the network of reporters who are able to cover this specialised topic.

Baker and McKenzie wrote the stories for Fairfax, which publishes predominantly into the Sydney and Melbourne markets, but not widely across Australia. The reporters wanted the coverage to be national and, therefore, they attempted to collaborate with the ABC to expand their audience. Richard Baker explained the reason why Fairfax was willing to let the reporters establish a media outlet collaboration with the ABC to gain access to radio listeners and viewers Australia-wide.

> The ABC reaches a national audience. Often a lot of stuff now gets carried in the *[Sydney Morning] Herald* and the *Financial Review*, but that is still predominantly an eastern seaboard, or a Melbourne/ Sydney audience. I know the *Financial Review* is sold nationally but its sales are not huge. So [ABC coverage] just increases the size of the audience, and potentially finds a different audience. If the opportunity is there, why not take it? Why not give the story an extra zing-along?

The Fairfax/ABC Securency coverage reached a far wider audience than the print-based newspapers in south-eastern Australia alone would have done.

The investigation led eventually to prosecutions by the Commonwealth Director of Public Prosecutions (CDPP) of Securency International Pty Ltd and its currency printer Note Printing Australia for conspiracy to commit foreign bribery offences in Indonesia, Malaysia and Vietnam.[10] The two companies pleaded guilty and paid more than $21 million in pecuniary penalty orders.[11] In addition, the CEO of Securency pleaded guilty in 2012 to a charge of false accounting. An Indonesian agent of Securency pleaded guilty in 2013 to conspiracy to bribe foreign officials. Investigations and prosecutions continued over the following years. A former CEO of Securency pleaded guilty in 2018 to conspiracy to bribe foreign public officials in Indonesia and Malaysia. Securency's former business development manager pleaded guilty in 2018 to false accounting. A Securency banknote specialist pleaded guilty in 2018 to conspiracy to bribe foreign public officials in Malaysia.[12] Once all the prosecutions were completed in 2018, the journalists were finally able to disclose how the 10-year investigation had begun in 2008 with one whistleblower meeting them in a café.[13]

Award

Richard Baker and Nick McKenzie won a Walkley Award for Investigative Journalism in 2011 for their long-running investigation into Securency.

Case study 13: *Caldey Island abuse scandal*

A lawyer in England emailed me in 2017 to ask, if I would speak to a child abuse victim in Australia who had been abused in Wales as a child. The request came from Eli Ward's lawyer, Tracey Emmott. I agreed to have a talk with the whistleblower. Here was another example of an established trusting reporter-source relationship leading to further leads and potential investigations. The whistleblower was a woman who had already settled a class action in England but she was dissatisfied with the legal outcome and wanted to expose the behaviour of monks in a Catholic abbey on Caldey Island in Wales. As a child, the woman had been repeatedly sexually abused by a Catholic monk when she visited Caldey Island in Wales during the 1980s while on holiday with her parents. The girl later moved with her family to Australia and settled in Newcastle in New South Wales. She reported the abuse as a teenager to her deputy principal, but her school failed to report the crimes to the police in Australia or in Wales. Instead, the deputy principal said a prayer with her and told her she didn't need to talk about the offences again. As an adult, she became very distressed by the many media reports of sexual abuse in religious organisations being reported, especially by the *Newcastle Herald*, and began searching online for a lawyer who might represent her in the UK. Her search terms revealed the Waddington investigation and the name of Eli Ward's lawyer, Tracey Emmott. The victim made contact with the lawyer and with other girls she knew had also been victims of her offender. Six of the victims – now women – joined in a group civil action seeking compensation for personal injury from the abuse by the monk, Thaddeus Kotik. The victims were statute-barred from legal action due to the Statute of Limitations that then applied to personal injury cases, but they received very small *ex gratia* payments. My contact, who was the lead plaintiff, wanted to expose Caldey Abbey's concealment of the paedophile in the Abbey and the Abbey's failure over decades to report the offender to the police whilst continuing to enable him to offend against children.

Over the following few months, I used Skype to conduct face-to-face interviews with the victims and their parents who were scattered between Australia, the UK and Asia. I offered the story to the *Guardian* which had opened its Australian bureau. An Australian bureau meant I could file copy directly to the features editor in Sydney, who then forwarded the story and photos directly to the London office for publication in the UK. The *modus operandi* of the priest indicated he was a prolific offender, so there was potential to find other victims if they could contact me directly. The newspaper agreed to tag the story with my email address so that other victims could make contact directly.[14] Once the story was published, both the reader and the media reaction in the UK was overwhelming. Several more victims came forward.[15] After years of public denial of the offending, the pressure of publicity forced the Abbot to finally apologise for failing to report the offender to the police.[16]

After the initial story was published, the reader reaction meant I needed someone on the ground in Wales to follow up leads on location. The *Guardian* asked their religion writer Harriet Sherwood and their Wales correspondent Steve Morris to assist me. Meanwhile, BBC Wales and ITV picked up the story and ran television and radio news stories. BBC Wales and ITV both interviewed me via Skype for their television news bulletins from my desk in Australia. BBC Wales asked if they could collaborate with me on the story. A collaboration agreement was made with the *Guardian* and BBC Radio Wales that I would file breaking stories to the *Guardian* and that these would be published before the radio stories were broadcast. However, we agreed that I would send audio grabs to BBC Wales in advance of publication so the news team had time to revoice the audio grabs to ensure the anonymity of the victims, and be ready to broadcast as soon as the stories were published. Radio Wales Assistant News Editor Lorraine Walsh strongly backed the investigation and personally revoiced the words of the victims to ensure anonymity. For the collaboration to work, there needed to be a high level of trust between all three parties to the collaboration. Everyone abided by the embargo agreements and the collaboration continued for several weeks.

The story ramped up substantially a week after the first exposé when more whistleblowers came forward and revealed that a convicted sex offender, who had been on the run from the police for seven years, had been living in the abbey on Caldey Island until 2011.[17] More victims of Kotik also came forward. One of the plaintiffs, who had fled the UK to escape the trauma of her childhood memories, spoke about how the abuse had ruined her life.[18] Another victim of Kotik, Joanna Biggs came forward, this time waiving her right to anonymity, because she needed answers about the suspicious drowning death of her younger sister Theresa Biggs, aged 6, on the island in 1977.[19] In early 2018, the first male victim of Kotik came forward. He wanted to go to Caldey Island as a way of resolving his childhood memories. I went to the UK in the northern summer of 2018, met my colleague Steve Morris and together we accompanied the male victim to Caldey Island and walked with him to the monastery, the chocolate factory, the lighthouse and other locations where he had been taken by the offender.[20]

Joanna Biggs was determined that the truth about her sister's drowning death should be exposed. She obtained a copy of the inquest file and sent it to me. The statements in the file from three teenage boys who had tried to rescue Theresa indicated a nun had allowed the child to swim in very dangerous conditions. Theresa's father, who had attended the inquest two days after his daughter drowned in 1977, was able to confirm that several of the statements in the file had not been presented at the inquest. The coroner's omission of the statements by the boys meant that the statement of the nun, Sister Sheila Singleton, was accepted by the coroner, laying blame on Theresa for allegedly swimming without permission when this was not true.

Joanna's own childhood memory was that the nun had allowed her sister to swim and had helped put inflatable arm bands on her. Joanna's knowledge of what happened was finally vindicated by the evidence of the statements of the boys who had tried to rescue the little girl in perilous conditions. The inquest delivered findings that were not consistent with the facts. In addition, a Catholic priest, who signed as the witness to the statements of the teenage boys and thus knew the true circumstances that implicated the nun, was the Church representative who visited Theresa's parents over several years to comfort and counsel them over their daughter's death. The priest was promoted to a senior position in the Church. Upon discovering the concealed statements, the family of Theresa Biggs sought a review of the inquest findings.

During my trip to Wales in 2018 I was invited to stay with the parents of Theresa Biggs on 17 July. That evening I was able to explain to the parents the full circumstances of their daughter's death. When the parents woke on 18 July, the 41st anniversary of their daughter's death, they were finally aware of what had really happened and why; and they knew for the first time that their daughter was not to blame for her own death. The parents, by then in their 80s, were extraordinarily relieved. The revelation of the truth began that day to mend the relationship between Joanna and her parents, who had been betrayed for four decades. In October 2018, the Attorney-General for England and Wales overturned the findings of the 1977 inquest based on the obvious contradictions between the evidence presented to the inquest and the findings handed down. Theresa Biggs was officially absolved of the false blame attributed to her by the nun who took the group of children swimming in dangerous conditions.[21]

Caldey Island abuse victims were invited to contribute to the Independent Inquiry into Child Sexual Abuse's (IICSA's) Truth Project. The victims submitted a substantial joint document to IICSA and have called for the Welsh National Assembly to establish a Government Inquiry.

Case study 14: *Luxembourg leaks*

Following the tax haven investigation, the ICIJ received another leak in 2014, this time of 28,000 tax files of some of the world's largest multinational companies.[22] The volume of documents could not easily have been leaked as physical paper, as one of the reporters explained: "It is a very modern journalistic story, one that might never have come about if a person had had to carry several heavy boxes out of an office."[23] The leaked documents implicated a former prime minister of Luxembourg who held a powerful position in the European Union. The ICIJ published almost 550 Luxembourg tax rulings that were signed and stamped by the country's officials. The rulings published online were searchable and available to the public. The investigation also revealed that the newly installed European Commission president Jean-Claude Juncker had been instrumental in establishing corporate tax avoidance schemes when he had been prime minister of Luxembourg. Even though the deals were legal, they were morally indefensible.

> It was an awkward revelation for someone who had come to the EU post acknowledging that his commission had to win back the trust of EU citizens or fail. The more awkward, because the political tide has changed in recent years. While such deals may be perfectly legal, they are seen as morally untenable in the context of austerity and high unemployment in Europe.[24]

The key to the political impact of the story was that many media outlets published the story simultaneously in 26 countries.[25] The series of reports, dubbed LuxLeaks, detailed how 343 companies including IKEA, Deutsche Bank and Apple paid little or no tax in the countries where they were based, by channelling profits through the Grand Duchy of Luxembourg, a country with a population of under 700,000 people.[26] The ICIJ published the tax rulings on its website, making them public and searchable.[27] As the stories by ICIJ reporters began to roll out in the Luxembourg leaks coverage, governments and the European Commission were forced to act. Banking secrecy, which had been the norm in Luxembourg, was challenged. The European Commission announced probes into at least two companies, Amazon and Fiat, that had obtained tax rulings in Luxembourg. It also opened infringement procedures against Luxembourg, claiming that the authorities had refused to provide all of the documents that the Commission had requested.[28]

Case study 15: The Panama and Paradise Papers

The Panama Papers

An ICIJ investigation into the activities of Panama-based global law firm Mossack Fonseca by 370 ICIJ reporters culminated in 2016 in coordinated coverage by more than 100 news organisations around the world in the largest cross-border collaboration ever undertaken (Berglez and Gearing 2018). The basis for the investigation was a leak of 11.5 million documents known as the Panama Papers, which revealed political leaders, extremely wealthy individuals and companies had created 214,000 shell companies to hide off-shore assets, launder money and avoid paying tax.[29] The files related to people and companies in more than 200 countries and territories and spanned almost 40 years, from the late 1970s until the end of 2015.[30] Mossack Fonseca closed in March 2018, blaming its closure on reputational damage caused by the revelations about its role in global tax evasion in the Panama Papers.

The Panama Papers won many journalism prizes including the Pulitzer Prize in 2017 for explanatory reporting.[31]

The Paradise Papers

In 2016, a smaller cache of 1.4TB of electronic data files was leaked to a German newspaper. The leak of 14.3 million documents became the source data for an investigation by 381 journalists in 67 countries that produced global coverage rolled out by 95 collaborating media outlets (Hopkins and Bengtsson 2017). The documents detailed individual and company financial transactions exposing tax minimisation schemes by celebrities, royalty and global companies such as Facebook, Apple, Disney, Uber, Nike, Walmart, Allianz, Siemens, McDonald's and Yahoo. The nickname of the database, Paradise Papers, refers to the exotic locations where individuals and companies created entities to minimise their tax liability (Berglez and Gearing 2018). The leak included documents from Bermuda law firm Appleby and government records of corporate registries in 19 countries, including Antigua and Barbuda, Aruba, the Bahamas, Barbados, Bermuda, the Cayman Islands, the Cook Islands, Dominica, Granada, Labuan, Lebanon, Malta, the Marshall Islands, St Kitts and Nevis, St Lucia, St Vincent, Samoa, Trinidad and Tobago and Vanuatu (Hopkins and Bengtsson 2017). The investigation required the reporters to find connections between companies in their own and other countries, verifying the links between people and companies that had operated behind a cyber screen of secrecy.

Organisational collaboration in investigative journalism

The case studies in this chapter demonstrate some of the extraordinary potential for investigative reporters who are able to build networks of connection, to verify the authenticity of data and plan and undertake both small and large collaborations that produce exclusive media coverage that is rolled out across multiple media platforms. Each investigation is a manifestation of the nascent global fourth estate that is capable of highlighting injustice and having problems addressed at the national, international and global level. The increasing connectedness, or hyper-connectedness, in the networked society has resulted in journalists increasingly adopting the global *outlook,* described by Peter Berglez. Rather than categorising issues as discretely national or international and viewing them from a nationalistic perspective, issues are viewed instead from a global perspective (Berglez 2013). This transformation in perspective recognises the present and future interdependence of nations.

The advent of the network society, moreover, is disrupting the competitive nature of media outlets in seeking exclusivity. Now that audiences can source news easily and cheaply from anywhere, organisational collaboration has become a potential benefit. Media outlets are collaborating to share investigation costs; to speed up investigations; to reach a wider cross-media audience; and to increase the political impact of a story. Collaborations are being instigated by reporters and are being formed with some of the most powerful global media outlet mastheads. The collaborations in this book were experimental, but in the years since they were undertaken, the reporters and media outlets have continued to collaborate, breaking more powerful socio-political stories using the same techniques. Thus we see that social media platforms and Web based communication technologies are together facilitating communication: (i) between journalists and their news contacts; (ii) between journalists and audiences; (iii) between journalists and their media outlets (especially when the reporters are working out of office or overseas); and (iv) between audiences and media outlets.

Collaboration is still perceived as a radical departure from lone wolf investigative journalism. Even the ICIJ director Gerard Ryle was initially reluctant to collaborate because of the perceived risks, but he saw the need for more manpower to analyse, verify and write about his first leaked database. Walker Guevara explained the reluctance of the ICIJ to collaborate and their decision to do so because they could not see any other option. The resulting collaboration linked reporters in 58 countries with the ICIJ headquarters in Washington and once the initial reluctance was overcome, trusted journalists were joined into a network of reporters who were working for major media outlets in many countries. Once those media outlets decided to collaborate, the benefits of working together became more tangible. Collaboration is now accepted to be a driving force that can help the news ecosystem to survive the financial constraints caused by digital disruption.[32] The US Center for Cooperative Media has defined six models of collaborative journalism in which collaborations are established for a temporary project or as an ongoing collaboration. Each type of collaboration has different levels of sharing, ranging from sharing data and story ideas at the deepest level of collaboration to working together to create content, to creating content separately and sharing the distribution of the content (Stonbely 2017).

Benefits of organisational collaboration

Three main benefits of organisational collaboration are revealed in this research: financial/economic benefits; improved audience impact and longevity of coverage; and greater political and social impact. For some investigations, only one of the benefits may be realised while for others, two or more of the benefits are evident.

Financial/economic benefits

The major benefits of collaboration are savings in the most limited commodities in newsgathering: time and money. In the ICIJ tax haven investigation, it would have been prohibitively expensive for a journalist or even a group of journalists from one country to travel to more than 40 countries to carry out the investigation. The international collaboration sped up the investigation by a significant factor and vastly reduced the cost. Transnational cooperation in journalism in this case enabled media outlets to retain and capitalise on the local exclusivity of their stories whilst at the same time benefiting from the collective work of many reporters and therefore being able to deliver domestic stories with a transnational context (Konow-Lund, Gearing and Berglez 2019).

Improved audience impact and longevity of coverage

The greater the impact of a news report and the longer it remains visible to audiences, the greater the potential political and social change it can achieve. Radio and television, which convey the voice or footage of news sources directly to audiences have a higher potential impact on audiences; however, both of these media have lacked longevity until the advent of digital archiving and retrieval. Online archiving of radio and television news coverage now gives audiences the ability to have permanent access.

Physical newspapers have been recognised in the past as wielding the strongest political power even though they cannot convey the voice or footage of news sources but only quotations from news sources in black and white. Equally, the ability of newspaper coverage to also be archived online and to remain accessible and easily searchable may mean newspapers retain their position of having pre-eminent political impact.

Greater political and social impact

While time and cost considerations are significant reasons to instigate collaboration between media outlets, sometimes the main reason to collaborate is to enable an issue to be canvassed in the public sphere by gathering a larger audience. The ICIJ tax haven investigation resulted in agenda items addressing tax evasion being added to the G20 Leaders' Summit in Brisbane in November 2014. This was significant because the G20 represents 20 nations or groups of nations (such as the European Union) and accounts for 85 per cent of the world economy, 76 per cent of global trade and two-thirds of the world's population (Australian Government 2014). ICIJ director Gerard Ryle believes the digital era heralds a new golden age of journalism (Posetti 2015). In tracing the ICIJ's LuxLeaks investigation, *Irish Times* reporter Colm Keena made a strong case for the potential that journalists will have on the global stage if they engage with and use technology to call the powerful to account.

> The structures detailed in the LuxLeaks files – groups of companies swapping huge amounts of money in complex financial manoeuvres – are themselves products of the internet age. So is the phenomenon of global scoops based on databanks that journalists could once only have dreamed of.
>
> (Keena 2014)

In summary, the benefits of network building by media outlets in the networked media environment are financial savings; improved audience impact and longevity of coverage; wider distribution and thus greater political and social impact. Nevertheless, there is not expected to be a headlong adoption of collaboration between media organisations because they are ultimately businesses in a competition to survive under increasingly difficult economic conditions.

Notes

1 Marina Walker Guevara. 2013. "How we all survived likely the largest collaboration in journalism history." ICIJ: *The Global Muckraker*, 12 April 2013.
2 News and feature coverage: 10 May 2013: S. O'Neill, M. McKenna and A. Gearing. 2013. "Former Archbishop of York 'covered up' sex abuse scandal." *The Times*; M. McKenna, A. Gearing and S. O'Neill. 2013. "Child sex scandal in two countries rocks Anglican Church." ICIJ: *The Australian*; S. O'Neill. 2013. "Victim of clergyman's abuse was groomed as young chorister." *The Times;* and M. McKenna and A. Gearing. 2013. "Church's wall of silence on sexual abuse." ICIJ: *The Australian*, 10 May 2013.
3 *The Times*. 2013. "Leading article: action this day." London, News UK: *The Times*. 10 May 2013. www.thetimes.co.uk/tto/opinion.
4 Lucy Manning. 2013. "Former choirboy issues C of E abuse cover-up claims." London, *ITV News.* 10 May 2013. https://www.itv.com/news/2013-05-10/former-choirboy-issues-cofe-abuse-cover-up-claims.
5 Sean O'Neill. 2013. "Church details Inquiry into alleged sex abuse cover-up." London, News UK: *The Times*. 22 July 2013. www.bishop-accountability.org.
6 Sean O'Neill. 2018. "Sean O'Neill on the problems with his cancer treatment." London, News UK: *The Times,* 12 May 2018. https://www.thetimes.co.uk.
7 Richard Baker and Nick McKenzie. 2018. "How a meeting in a café with a journalist prompted Australia's biggest foreign bribery case." Sydney, Fairfax: *Sydney Morning Herald*. 30 November 2018. https://www.smh.com.au.
8 Cover Up. 2013. *Four Corners.* ABC Television. 30 September 2013. https://www.abc.net.au.
9 Cover Up. 2013. *Four Corners.* ABC Television. 30 September 2013. https://www.abc.net.au.
10 CDPP. 2018–2019. "Securency and Note Printing Australia foreign bribery prosecutions finalised." Canberra, Commonwealth Director of Public Prosecutions. https://www.cdpp.gov.au.
11 CDPP. 2018–2019. "Securency and Note Printing Australia foreign bribery prosecutions finalised." Canberra, Commonwealth Director of Public Prosecutions. https://www.cdpp.gov.au.
12 CDPP. 2018–2019. "Securency and Note Printing Australia foreign bribery prosecutions finalised.! Canberra, Commonwealth Director of Public Prosecutions. https://www.cdpp.gov.au.
13 Richard Baker and Nick McKenzie. 2018. "How a meeting in a cafe with a journalist prompted Australia's biggest foreign bribery case." Sydney, Nine: *Sydney Morning Herald*. 30 November 2018. https://www.smh.com.au.
14 Amanda Gearing. 2017. "Revealed: monk who abused children on 'crime free' Caldey Island for decades." London, Guardian Media Group: *Guardian*. 18 November 2017. https://www.theguardian.com.
15 Amanda Gearing and Harriet Sherwood. 2017. "Three more women allege abuse by Caldey Island monk." London, Guardian Media Group: *Guardian*. 22 November 2017. https://www.theguardian.com.
16 Steve Morris and Amanda Gearing. 2017. "Caldey Island abbot apologises over failure to report abuse claims." London, Guardian Media Group: *Guardian*. 23 November 2017. https://www.theguardian.com.

17 Amanda Gearing and Steve Morris. 2017. "Sex offender hid in Caldey Island abbey for seven years." London, Guardian Media Group: *Guardian*. 25 November 2017. https://www.theguardian.com.

18 Amanda Gearing and Steve Morris. 2017. "Woman abused by Caldey Island monk tells of lasting impact." London, Guardian Media Group: *Guardian*. 5 December 2017. https://www.theguardian.com.

19 Steve Morris and Amanda Gearing. 2017. "Woman abused as a child by Caldey Island monk waives right to anonymity." London, Guardian Media Group: *Guardian*. 5 December 2017. https://www.theguardian.com.

20 Amanda Gearing and Steve Morris. 2018. "Caldey Island victim: 'It should be given over to the National Trust.'" London, Guardian Media Group: *Guardian*. 21 July 2018. https://www.theguardian.com.

21 Amanda Gearing and Steve Morris. 2018. "'I've got finality,' says abuse victim pressing for new inquest into sister's death." London, Guardian Media Group: *Guardian*. 16 October 2018. https://www.theguardian.com.

22 Simon Bowers. 2014. "Luxembourg tax files: how tiny state rubber-stamped tax avoidance on an industrial scale." London, Guardian Media Group: *Guardian*. https://www.theguardian.com.

23 Colm Keena. 2014. "LuxLeaks: a very modern scoop." Dublin, Irish Times Trust: *Irish Times*. 8 November 2014. www.irishtimes.com.

24 Honor Mahony. 2014. "LuxLeaks: an opportunity?" Brussels, EUobserver. com: *EuObserver*. 2 January 2014. https://euobserver.com.

25 Leslie Wayne, Kelly Carr, Marina Walker Guevara, Mar Cabra and Michael Hudson. 2014. "Leaked documents expose global companies' secret tax deals in Luxembourg." ICIJ. https://www.icij.org.

26 Honor Mahony. 2014. "LuxLeaks: an opportunity?" Brussels, EUobserver. com: *EuObserver*. 2 January 2014. https://euobserver.com.

27 Caruana Galizia, Matthew, Mar Cabra, Margot Williams, Emilia Díaz-Struck and Hamish Boland Rudder. 2014. "Explore the documents: Luxembourg leaks database." Washington, DC: ICIJ.

28 Marina Walker Guevara. 2014. "Luxembourg leaks: a case study in collaborative journalism." ICIJ: *The Global Muckraker*, 6 November 2014. www.icij.org.

29 ICIJ. 2016. "The Panama Papers: giant leak of offshore financial records exposes global array of crime and corruption." USA: ICIJ. https://www.icij.org/investigations/panama-papers.

30 ICIJ. 2016. A new ICIJ investigation exposes a rogue offshore industry. Washington: ICIJ. https://www.icij.org/investigations/panama-papers/new-icij-investigation-exposes-rogue-offshore-industry.

31 Melody Kramer. 2017. "Journalists around the world are working together more than ever. Here are 56 examples." Florida, Poynter Institute. 12 April 2017. https://www.poynter.org/reporting-editing/2017/journalists-around-the-world-are-working-together-more-than-ever-here-are-56-examples.

32 Melody Kramer. 2017." "Journalists around the world are working together more than ever. Here are 56 examples." Florida, Poynter Institute. 12 April 2017. https://www.poynter.org/reporting-editing.

8 Coronavirus, a global story

The first day of January 2020 was the first whole day that the World Health Organisation knew that there was a severe new disease, with an unknown cause, in China. Journalists covering this story had a complex task to achieve, conveying what was happening in the real world and providing reliable health information from official sources, who, at first, did not have clear information. Journalists in every country needed to look overseas, first to China where the pandemic originated, and then to other countries, to see how differently the governments and health systems were responding. The global implications of the virus required journalists to report on the global nature of the health crisis, as well as monitoring those countries that had been infected days or weeks earlier, to be able to report on the possible trajectory of infections, hospitalisations and deaths. In addition, the COVID-19 crisis was not only a health crisis: it was a multi-dimensional crisis affecting freedom of movement, supply chains, the travel and tourism industries, national and the global economies, national and global politics and diplomacy. The speed with which the world as we knew it seemed to unravel was staggering. The word 'unprecedented' was applied to much that happened in 2020.

In Australia, record-breaking intense and widespread bushfires were capturing national and world attention. Media attention centred on Mallacoota Beach on New Year's Eve, 31 December 2019, where residents fled to the ocean as flames from intense and fast-moving bushfires turned the sky red, swapping day for night in apocalyptic scenes. On the same day, the World Health Organisation was informed of a cluster of pneumonia cases of unknown cause, detected in Wuhan City in China.[1] Countries bordering China braced for potential infection transmission. On 3 January 2020, the Vietnamese Ministry of Health issued a directive to tighten quarantine along the 1,200 km border between China and Vietnam, fearing for their population of 100 million people (La et al.

DOI: 10.4324/9781003139980-8

2020). Four days later, on 7 January 2020, Chinese authorities identified the SARS-CoV-2 virus as the cause of the new illness.[2] The strange pneumonia was reported in the media from 9 January; and when the first case in Vietnam was identified on 23 January, incoming travellers were screened at airports, seaports and terrestrial borders (La et al. 2020). Similar dramatic and swift action was taken by many governments, but certainly not by all. In Vietnam, early and decisive action to minimise the transmission of the infection meant that, even though the country had a relatively poor medical system, infection rates and deaths were minimised by reliable provision of government health information, especially via social media such as Facebook and a local app Zalo, which has 100 million users (La et al. 2020). The value of timely and scientifically sound government action and prompt and accurate health messaging via mainstream and social media saved countless lives.

As time progressed, it became clear that governments adopted differing policies based – or not based – on the medical advice they were given. Reporters also had the task of comparing the differing consequences of policies that were adopted on the transmission of the virus, the death rate, the impact on health care systems, the impact on economies and mental health and many other variables. Although there have been many other global stories, this particular global story came with a potentially lethal illness and therefore had huge news impact. In addition, the story broke at a time when there was digital connection between the World Health Organisation and most countries of the world. Global data were collected daily from hospitals and health departments and released daily via a Coronavirus Disease dashboard providing league tables of new infection numbers, confirmed cases and deaths.[3] The pandemic became, in effect, a live global experiment that allowed residents in any country to compare effective and ineffective leadership and its consequences in terms of infection rates and death rates, for people in different countries or states. Reliable data enabled the media to challenge leaders and politicians in their own countries to potentially improve their responses to the pandemic.

Leadership

Decisive and responsive political leadership was vital to the speed with which governments were able to close their borders, order residents to isolate themselves and provide financial support to people who were ordered to stop work. Significant differences in outcomes became apparent in the first three months of the year with soaring virus transmission and death rates in some countries, such as the UK and the US, that had male leaders, compared with lower transmission and death rates in other countries, such as New Zealand and Germany, that had female leaders.[4] A study by British researchers compared COVID-19 responses by 194 male leaders with responses by 19 female leaders and found that in the first three months of 2020, death rates in female-led countries were half of those in male-led countries (Garikipati and Kambhampati 2020). The research found that countries led by women reacted more quickly and decisively, went into lockdown sooner and conducted more tests, resulting in lower infection and death rates (Garikipati and Kambhampati 2020). Male leaders, on the other hand, were found to take more risks with their own and others' health. British Prime Minister Boris Johnson, for example, went to a hospital and shook hands with infected patients and contracted the illness himself.[5]

While many countries aimed to 'flatten the curve' of infection, New Zealand aimed for eradication of the virus. New Zealand Prime Minister Jacinda Ardern was able to engage the population in a shared purpose of saving lives and minimising damage to the economy. Hallmarks of her leadership were accepting scientific and medical advice, mobilising collective effort and enabling people to cope (Wilson 2020). Interestingly, Jacinda Ardern used social media to give frequent and impromptu updates or messages of encouragement. Many of these messages were delivered from her home or from moving vehicles such as taxis or buses via mobile phone using Facebook Live. Her leadership style and effectiveness have been held up as a gold standard in minimising infection rates in the country. For example, New Zealand recorded 19 COVID-19 deaths to the end of April 2020 in a population of 4.8 million, compared with 1,190 deaths in Scotland at the same date, in a population of 4.9 million (Wilson 2020). Jacinda Ardern's messages attracted a strong following of New Zealanders as well as people from overseas who posted comments on the livestream in admiration of her leadership, and even inviting her to be the prime minister of their home countries. The public sphere has become globalised by digital technology: journalists must therefore adapt and go global in their networking and collaboration if they are to continue in their role as the domestic fourth estate and expand to become the global fourth estate. More and more domestic news stories have global dimensions, and only collaboration can reveal the entire scope of these stories.

Impact on the media

The financial impact in early 2020 of the COVID-19 outbreak on businesses around the globe reduced spending on media advertising, causing a very sudden collapse of newspapers and other media outlets. Ironically, this collapse occurred at a time when people most needed reliable, timely news and information about the developing pandemic. In the US 36,000 news staff were laid off or were paid reduced wages.[6] Many major publishers that had paywalls dropped their paywalls in the interests of public health, to allow free public access to their pandemic coverage.[7] Stretched newsrooms turned to collaboration as a means of covering the pandemic, sharing stories and cross-promoting COVID-19 coverage (Murray 2020). Online fact watchdog First Draft expanded its existing global collaboration for fighting misinformation and fake news and brought its partners together to work on the pandemic, creating tutorials and guides for responsible reporting.[8] In Australia, more than 200 regional newspapers closed or suspended their printed publications, many after being in operation for well over a century (Hess and Waller 2020). The impact of digital disruption on regional Australian newspapers was eclipsed suddenly and dramatically by the pandemic. As millions of people were ordered to stay at home or to work from home, digital face-to-face video conferencing software became vital. Daily downloads of video conferencing platform Zoom skyrocketed from 10 million in December 2019 to 200 million in March 2020 (Marks 2020). Reporting on the pandemic and other news, also went online. Many journalists worked from home and broadcast radio or television programmes from home. Within days of government isolation regulations, reporters had to convert from face-to-face, in-person newsgathering to online reporting with the aid of videoconferencing technologies. Television reporters used Zoom, Skype or other software to bring isolated news sources to their radio and television audiences. It is difficult to imagine how different the response would have been without social media, Web based communications and collaborations.

The pandemic fast-tracked the adoption of technologies and techniques used for investigative reporting. Reporters have been forced to report from isolation using social media networks to find and verify stories. They've been forced to use Web based communications technologies rather than in-person interviews. They've been forced suddenly into collaborations with other reporters as well as with other news outlets. The necessity of the changes, as well as the investment in technology to make the changes, means reporters who still have jobs are having to produce much more coverage with a much reduced budget. It is not clear yet what the new normal will be, but it is inconceivable that the technological and collaborative gains made are going to be unwound, even if COVID-19 becomes a preventable or treatable illness.

The global fourth estate

The work of the reporters cited in this book provides guides and inspiration for the current and next generations of journalists. The case studies show that robust investigative journalism is necessary to protect citizens in a democracy and, arguably, to protect the mechanisms that support democracy itself. Despite the large and sudden changes in the journalism field, there is evidence that high-quality investigative journalism will continue in some guise. Vivien Altman's prediction in 2014 was that:

> I do not believe that democracy can really survive without proper accountability and proper investigative journalism. I believe that the advent of social media and the changes to journalism will change things, but I believe that in terms of the importance of investigative journalism and functioning democracy, that it will survive.

Hopefully her prediction is true.

There is a strong link between the importance of investigative journalism and the maintenance of a healthy democracy. Castells has shown that the technological revolution is reshaping human society, creating economies which are interdependent – in effect a global society that is defined by its connections – a *network society* (Castells 2009). Each individual, according to Berglez, identifies and interacts with the *world* rather than identifying as belonging to a nation that interacts with other nations (Berglez 2013). He encourages journalists to adopt the same perspective and conceptualise stories globally. Global investigative journalism is not just a theory, but rather a practical way of working in the network society, finding, verifying and writing stories in any country or in several countries simultaneously. The analogue concepts of local, state, national and international news are far less relevant now than the borderless network society with its 24/7 news cycle that both breaks news and archives it, creating an easily accessible and searchable history of the world.

Investigative journalists who link with online networks have the potential to expand the range of voices that can be heard and the types of stories that can be told as they call the powerful to account and give voice to the voiceless. The evidence presented here indicates that media collaboration is strengthening the global fourth estate by enabling the reporting and wide publication of sensitive and controversial stories that could not have occurred previously. Collaborations have been demonstrated to be effective between regional and state-based newspapers, between cross-media outlets (such as newspaper and television), between major masthead newspapers in two or more different countries and between multiple media outlets simultaneously. Organisational collaboration enhances the political power of investigative new coverage by attracting much larger audiences.

Evidence for the financial necessity of organisational collaboration is compelling. Media outlets will no longer be able to afford or to justify international airfares and travel, chasing stories which could be achieved for a fraction of the cost by using digital tools and reporter and organisational collaboration. The biggest stories in journalism will, by definition, be global and will speak into the globalised public sphere. This movement will also push media practitioners to search for international and global links to stories which emerge in the domestic news sphere. The greatest synergies will become evident where technology enables a culture of sharing and where journalists cooperate with, rather than resist, this culture. It is in this scenario that journalists will be able to make the most of the opportunities which are being presented, as demonstrated in the case studies cited in this book.

Extending the research findings presented in this book to the profession at large has the potential to empower experienced and novice journalists. This research could be repeated usefully in other countries. Subsequent findings have the potential to inform the industry of additional new practices at a time of great uncertainty and very rapid change. The benefits of gathering new data over the next few years can be expected to be very beneficial to shaping how society views and endorses investigative journalism, and potentially how society views and endorses its commitment to democracy. A strong independent investigative journalism sector is crucial to the global community.

Notes

1   "Public statement for collaboration on COVID-19 vaccine development." 2020. World Health Organization. 13 April 2020. https://www.who.int/news.
2   "Public statement for collaboration on COVID-19 vaccine development." 2020. World Health Organization. 13 April 2020. https://www.who.int/news.
3   "WHO Coronavirus Disease (COVID-19) Dashboard." 2020. World Health Organization. https://covid19.who.int.
4   Avivah Wittenberg-Cox. 2020. "What do countries with the best Coronavirus responses have in common? Women leaders." New Jersey, *Forbes*. 13 April 2020. https://www.forbes.com.
5   Kate Proctor and Matthew Weaver. 2020. "'I shook hands with everybody,' says Boris Johnson weeks before coronavirus diagnosis." London, Guardian Media Group: *Guardian*. 28 March 2020. https://www.theguardian.com.

6 Marc Tracy. 2020. "News media outlets have been ravaged by the pandemic." 10 April 2020. New York, *New York Times*. https://www.nytimes.com.

7 Sara Jade. 2020. "Major publishers take down paywalls for coronavirus coverage." New York, *Adweek*. https://www.adweek.com.

8 Laura Garcia. 2020. "Covering Coronavirus: an online course for journalists." 1 April 2020. *First Draft.* https://firstdraftnews.org.

References

Abdenour, Jesse. 2017. "Digital gumshoes: Investigative journalists' use of social media in television news reporting." *Digital Journalism* 5: 472–492.

Aitamurto, Tanja. 2014. "Collective intelligence in journalism: Extended search, blended responsibility, and ruptured ideals." *Collective Intelligence*. Boston: MIT.

Alfter, Brigitte and Stefan Candea. 2019. "Cross-border collaborative journalism: New practice, new questions." *Journal of Applied Journalism & Media Studies* 8 (2): 141–149. doi:10.1386/ajms.8.2.141_1.

Australian Government. 2014. The G20. www.dfat.gov.au/trade/g20.

Bachelard, Michael. 2008. *Behind the Exclusive Brethren*. Carlton North, Australia: Scribe Publications.

Bacon, Wendy. 2011. "Investigative journalism in the academy—possibilities for storytelling across time and space." *Pacific Journalism Review* 17 (1): 45–66.

Barnhurst, Kevin. 2013. "Trust me, I'm an innovative journalist." In *Rethinking Journalism: Trust and Participation in a Transformed News Landscape*, edited by Chris Peters and Marcel Broersma, 210–220. London: Routledge.

Bennett, James. 2013. "Return to Dunalley – a family's survival story, six months on." In *7.30 Report*. Tasmania: ABC Television.

Berglez, Peter. 2008. "What is global journalism?" *Journalism Studies* 9 (6): 845–858.

Berglez, Peter 2013. *Global Journalism: Theory and Practice*. New York: Peter Lang.

Berglez, Peter and Amanda Gearing. 2018. "The Panama and Paradise Papers: The rise of a global fourth estate." *International Journal of Communication* 12: 4573–4592.

Bernstein, Carl and Bob Woodward. 1974. *All the President's Men*. New York: Simon & Schuster.

Bowden, Tracy. 2012. "Church abuse victims share stories before Royal Commission." In *7.30 Report*. Sydney: ABC Television.

Boyer, Dominic. 2013. *The Life Informatic: Newsmaking in the Digital Era*. London: Cornell University Press.

Bruns, Axel and Jean Burgess. 2012. "Researching news discussion on Twitter." *Journalism Studies* 13 (5–6): 801–814. doi:10.1080/1461670X.2012.664428. Accessed 26 June 2016.

Bruns, Axel, Jean Burgess, Kate Crawford and Frances Shaw. 2012. *#qldfloods and QPSMedia: Crisis Communication on Twitter in the 2011 South East Queensland Floods.* Brisbane: Centre of Excellence for Creative Industries and Innovation.

Cahill, Sally. 2014. *Inquiry into the Church of England's Response to Child Abuse Allegations.* UK: Church of England, Diocese of York.

Castells, Manuel. 1996. *The Rise of the Network Society.* Cambridge, MA: Blackwell.

Castells, Manuel. 2001. *The Internet Galaxy: Reflections on the Internet, Business, and Society.* Oxford: Oxford University Press.

Castells, Manuel. 2009. *The Information Age: Economy, Society, and Culture, Volume I: The Rise of the Network Society.* Hoboken, NJ: Wiley.

Castells, Manuel. 2011. "A network theory of power." *International Journal of Communication* 5: 773–787.

Cyranoski, David. 2020. "What China's coronavirus response can teach the rest of the world." *Nature* 579 (17 March): 479–480. doi:10.1038/d41586-020-00741-x.

Davies, Nick. 2009. *Flat Earth News: An Award-winning Reporter Exposes Falsehood, Distortion and Propaganda in the Global Media.* London: Vintage.

Deuze, M. 2005. "What is journalism?: Professional identity and ideology of journalists reconsidered." *Journalism* 6 (4): 442–464. doi:10.1177/1464884905056815.

Garikipati, Supriya and Uma Kambhampati. 2020. "Leading the fight against the pandemic: Does gender 'really' matter?" *Social Science Research Network* (3 June). https://papers.ssrn.com.

Gaynor, J. M. 2020. *Report of Inquiry under Division 4a of Part 4 of the Inspector-General of the Australian Defence Force Regulation 2016 into Questions of Unlawful Conduct Concerning the Special Operations Task Group in Afghanistan.* Canberra: Australian Defence Force.

Gearing, Amanda. 2012a. *Queensland Flood Collection 2011–2012 .* Brisbane: Queensland State Library.

Gearing, Amanda. 2012b. *The Torrent: Toowoomba and Lockyer Valley, January 2011.* Brisbane: University of Queensland Press.

Gearing, Amanda. 2013a. "Harnessing the power of real and virtual social networks during disasters." *The National Emergency Response* 26 (3 Winter): 8–11.

Gearing, Amanda. 2013b. "Why disaster survivors speak to reporters." *Australian Journalism Review* 35 (1): 71–81.

Gearing, Amanda. 2016. "Global investigative journalism in the network society." Doctor of Philosophy thesis, Department of Media, Entertainment and Creative Arts, Queensland University of Technology.

Gearing, Amanda. 2017. *The Torrent: A True Story of Heroism and Survival.* Brisbane: University of Queensland Press.

Gearing, Amanda. 2018. "Post-disaster recovery is a marathon, not a sprint: The need for a state sponsored recovery scheme." *Pacific Journalism Review* 24 (1): 70–87.

Gearing, Amanda. 2019. "Reporting disasters in the digital age." In *Ethical Reporting of Sensitive Topics*, edited by Ann Luce, 214–232. London: Routledge.

Gearing, Amanda and Peter Berglez. 2019. "The microcosm of global investigative journalism: Understanding cross-border connections beyond the ICIJ." *Journal of Applied Journalism & Media Studies* 8: 211–229. doi:10.1386/ajms.8.2.211_1.

Glaser, Mark. 2012. "Citizen journalism: Widening world views, extending democracy." In *The Routledge Companion to News and Journalism*, edited by Stuart Allan, 578–590. Abingdon: Routledge.

Goode, Luke. 2009. "Social news, citizen journalism and democracy." *New Media & Society* 11 (8): 1287–1305.

Green, Andrew. 2020. "Li Wenliang." *The Lancet* 395 (10225): 682.

Hamilton, James. 2016. *Democracy's Detectives: The Economics of Investigative Journalism*. Cambridge, MA: Harvard University Press.

Hanusch, Folker. 2015. "Transformative times: Australian journalists' perceptions of changes in their work." *Media International Australia, Incorporating Culture & Policy* 155 (1): 38–53.

Henley, Jon, Katharine Viner, Lee Glendining, Madhvi Pankhania, Francesca Panettas, Jonathan Richards and Mustafa Khalil. 2013. "Firestorm." *Guardian Australia* 23 May.

Hess, Kristy and Lisa Jane Waller. 2020. "Local newspapers and coronavirus: Conceptualising connections, comparisons and cures." *Media International Australia*. https://journals.sagepub.com/doi/abs/10.1177/1329878X20956455. doi:10.1177/1329878x20956455.

Hopkins, Nick and Helena Bengtsson. 2017. "What are the Paradise Papers and what do they tell us?" *The Guardian* 7 November.

Hyun, Ki Deuk. 2009. "Transnational convergence or national idiosyncrasies of Web-based political communication: A comparative analysis of network structures of political blogospheres in Germany, Great Britain, and the United States." Austin: The University of Texas.

Jay, Alexis, Malcolm Evans, Ivor Frank and Drusilla Sharpling. 2020. *The Anglican Church: Safeguarding in the Church of England and the Church in Wales, Investigation Report*. London: Independent Inquiry into Child Sexual Abuse.

Kapitan, Sommer. 2020. "The Facebook prime minister: How Jacinda Ardern became New Zealand's most successful political influencer." *The Conversation* 4 September. https://theconversation.com/the-facebook-prime-minister-how-jacinda-ardern-bcame-new-zealands-most-successful-political-influencer-144485.

Keane, John. 2010. *The Life and Death of Democracy*. London: Pocket.

Keena, Colm. 2014. "Luxleaks: A very modern scoop." *The Irish Times* 8 November. www.irishtimes.com/business/media-and-marketing/luxleaks-a-very-modern-scoop-1.1992293.

Konow-Lund, Maria, Amanda Gearing and Peter Berglez. 2019. "Transnational cooperation in journalism." In *Oxford Research Encyclopedia of Communication*. Oxford University Press. https://acrefore-9780190228613-e-881?rskey=7UjO7J&result=1.

Kovach, Bill and Tom Rosenstiel. 2014. *The Elements of Journalism: What Newspeople Should Know and the Public Should Expect*. Revised and updated 3rd ed. New York: Three Rivers Press.

La, V.-P., T.-H. Pham, M.-T. Ho, M.-H. Nguyen, K.-L. Nguyen, T.-T. Vuong, H.-K. T. Nguyen *et al.* 2020. "Policy response, social media and science journalism for the sustainability of the public health system amid the COVID-19 outbreak: The Vietnam lessons." *Sustainability* 12 (7): 2931–2958.

Lashmar, Paul. 2020. *Spies, Spin and the Fourth Estate: British Intelligence and the Media*. Edinburgh: Edinburgh University Press.

Leigh, David. 2019. *Investigative Journalism: A Survival Guide*. London: Palgrave Macmillan.

Luce, Ann. 2019. "Reporting suicide." In *Ethical Reporting of Sensitive Topics*, edited by Ann Luce, 70–94. London: Routledge.

Marks, Paul. 2020. "News: Virtual collaboration in the age of the coronavirus." *Association for Computing Machinery* 63 (9): 21–23. doi:10.1145/3409803.

McChesney, Robert and Victor Pickard. 2011. *Will the Last Reporter Please Turn Out the Lights: The Collapse of Journalism and What can be Done to Fix It*. New York, NY: The New Press.

McNair, Brian. 2003. *An Introduction to Political Communication*. 3rd ed. London: Routledge.

McNair, Brian. 2009. "Journalism and democracy." In *The Handbook of Journalism Studies*, edited by Karin Wahl-Jorgensen and Thomas Hanitzsch, 237–249. New York and Abingdon: Taylor & Francis.

McNair, Brian. 2014. "The media as political actors." In *Political Communication*, edited by C. Reinemann, 289–304. Berlin: De Gruyter Mouton.

Meldrum-Hanna, Caro. 2015. "Jail for journalism: Truth-telling and the first casualties of war." In *Media Talk*. Sydney: State Library of NSW.

Milton, John. 1644. "Areopagitica." In *Areopagitica: A Speech of Mr John Milton for the Liberty of Unlicenc'd Printing*, 1–40. London: Unnamed. https://quod.lib.umich.edu/e/eebo/a50883.0001.001/3?page=root;size=125;view=text.

Moon, Soo Jung and Patrick Hadley. 2014. "Routinizing a new technology in the newsroom: Twitter as a news source in mainstream media." *Journal of Broadcasting & Electronic Media* 58 (2): 289–305.

Murray, Stephanie. 2020,16 March. "How journalists are working together to cover the COVID-19 pandemic." In *Center for Cooperative Media*. https://www.niemanlab.org/2020/03/how-journlists-are-working-together-to-cover-the-covid-19-pandemic.

Nicholas, David, Peter Williams, Helen Martin and Peter Cole. 1998. *The Media and the Internet: Final Report of the British Library Funded Research Project 'The Changing Information Environment.'* London: The Association for Information Management.

Oh, Onook, Manish Agrawal and H. Raghav Rao. 2013. "Community intelligence and social media services: A rumor theoretical analysis of tweets during social crises." *MIS Quarterly* 37 (2): 407–424.

Pilger, John, ed. 2011. *Tell Me No Lies: Investigative Journalism and Its Triumphs.* London: Vintage Books.

Posetti, Julie. 2015. "Source protection erosion: A global case study on the rising threat to investigative journalism." In Medium.com. https://medium.com/@juieposetti/it-s-back-to-the-dark-car-park-for-many-investigative-journalists-f098ca569e46.

Posetti, Julie, Emily Bell and Pete Brown. 2020. *Journalism and the Pandemic: A Global Snapshot.* Washington, DC: International Center for Journalists.

Ray, Greg. 2013. "The Ocean is broken." *Newcastle Herald* 18 October.

Rosenthal, Robert. 2011,16 September. "New investigative reporting models: Opportunities and challenges." Back to the Source: ACIJ Investigative Journalism Conference. University of Technology Sydney, Sydney. https://www.youtube.com/watch?v=YdVCl4iD6CA.

Royal Commission into Institutional Responses to Child Sexual Abuse. 2017. *Criminal Justice Report.* Sydney: Australian Government.

Ryle, Gerard. 2013. *MEAA Centenary Lecture.* Brisbane: The Walkley Foundation.

Ryle, Gerard, Marina Walker Guevara, Michael Hudson, Nicky Hager, Duncan Campbell and Stefan Candea. 2013, 15 October. "Secret files expose offshore's global impact." In *Secrecy for Sale: Inside the Global Offshore Money Maze.* USA: International Consortium of Investigative Journalists.

Slaughter, Autumn and Bradley Brummel, Susan Drevo and Elana Newman. 2017. *Journalists and Safety Training: Experiences and Opinions.* USA: Dart Center for Journalism and Trauma. https://dartcenter.org/resources.

Sofronoff, Walter. 2015. *Grantham Floods Commission of Inquiry 2015.* Brisbane: Queensland Government.

Spyridou, Lia-Paschalia, Maria Matsiola, Andreas Veglis, George Kalliris and Charalambos Dimoulas. 2013. "Journalism in a state of flux: Journalists as agents of technology innovation and emerging news practices." *International Communication Gazette* 75 (1): 76–98.

Stonbely, Sarah. 2017. *Comparing Models of Collaborative Journalism.* Montclair, NJ: Center for Cooperative Media. https://collaborativejournalism.org/models.

Walker Guevara, Marina. 2014. "Luxembourg leaks: A case study in collaborative journalism." *The Global Muckraker* 6 November. http://www.icij.org/blog.

Ward, S. J. A. 2005. *The Invention of Journalism Ethics: The Path to Objectivity and Beyond.* Montreal, Canada: McGill-Queen's University Press.

Wilson, Suze. 2020. "Pandemic leadership: Lessons from New Zealand's approach to COVID-19." *Leadership* 16 (3): 279–293. doi:10.1177/1742715020929151.

Index